YORK NOTES

ANITA AND ME

MEERA SYAL

NOTES BY STEVE EDDY

PEARSON

YORK PRESS

YORK PRESS
322 Old Brompton Road, London SW5 9JH

PEARSON EDUCATION LIMITED
Edinburgh Gate, Harlow,
Essex CM20 2JE, United Kingdom
Associated companies, branches and representatives throughout the world

First published 2016

10 9 8 7 6 5 4 3 2 1

ISBN 978–1–2921–3803–9

Illustrations by Jeff Anderson; and Moreno Chiacchiera (page 61 only)

Phototypeset by Swales and Willis Ltd

Printed in Slovakia

Photo credits: © iStock/nullplus for page 8 / Africa Studio/Shutterstock for page 9 / © iStock/Holger Mette for page 11 / © iStock/Richard Goodrich for page 12 / smereka/Shutterstock for page 13 top / Rachel Duchesne/Shutterstock for page 13 bottom / Marek R.Swadzba/Shutterstock for page 15 top / © iStock/mikeuk for page 15 bottom / KAMONRAT/Shutterstock for page 16 / Dipak Shelare/Shutterstock for page 19 / Shyamalam uralinath/Shutterstock for page 21 / IMAGEPAST/Alamy for page 22 / Ramon Carretero/Shutterstock for page 25 middle / Photographee.eu/Shutterstock for page 25 bottom / © iStock/Mlenny Photography for page 27 / mb-fotos/Thinkstock for page 28 / Rosa Jay/Shutterstock for page 31 / effe45/Shutterstock for page 32 / Anastasija Popova/Shutterstock for page 33 / Wim Verhagen/Shutterstock for page 36 / Anirut Thailand/Shutterstock for page 39 / © iStock/Goddard_Photography for page 40 / Oleksandr Lytvynenko/ Shutterstock for page 41 / © iStock/RomoloTavani for page 42 / Lee O'Dell/ Shutterstock for page 47 / Michel Piccaya/Shutterstock for page 48 / Dario Vuksanovic/Shutterstock for page 51 / autsawin uttisin/Shutterstock for page 52 / Brian A Jackson/Shutterstock for page 54 / © iStock/Antonio Gravante for page 55 / meawnamacat/Shutterstock for page 56 / Bennian/Shutterstock for page 57 / GL Portrait/Alamy for page 58 top / © iStock/helovi for page 58 bottom / dnaveh/ Shutterstock for page 59 / Walter Kopplinger/Shutterstock for page 60 / LanKS/ Shutterstock for page 63 / © iStock/Pixonaut for page 64 / Gallo Images/Alamy for page 66 / Raymond Jones/Shutterstock for page 67/ Jupiterimage/Thinkstock for page 68 / yavuzunlu/Shutterstock for page 70 / © iStock/Steve Deben for page 79

CONTENTS

PART FOUR:
THEMES, CONTEXTS AND SETTINGS

PART FIVE:
FORM, STRUCTURE AND LANGUAGE

PART SIX:
PROGRESS BOOSTER ★

PART SEVEN:
FURTHER STUDY AND ANSWERS

PREPARING FOR ASSESSMENT

HOW WILL I BE ASSESSED ON MY WORK ON *ANITA AND ME*?

All exam boards are different, but whichever course you are following, your work will be examined through at least three of these four Assessment Objectives:

Assessment Objectives	Wording	Worth thinking about ...
AO1	Read, understand and respond to texts. Students should be able to: • maintain a critical style and develop an informed personal response • use textual references, including quotations, to support and illustrate interpretations.	• How well do I know what happens, what people say, do etc.? • What do *I* think about the key ideas in the novel? • How can I support my viewpoint in a really convincing way? • What are the best quotations to use and when should I use them?
AO2 *	Analyse the language, form and structure used by a writer to create meanings and effects, using relevant subject terminology where appropriate.	• What specific things does the writer 'do'? What choices has Syal made (why this particular word, phrase or paragraph here? Why does this event happen at this point?) • What effects do these choices create? Suspense? Sympathy? Humour?
AO3 *	Show understanding of the relationships between texts and the contexts in which they were written.	• What can I learn about society from the novel? (What does it tell me about race relations in the 1970s, for example?) • What was society like in the early 1970s? Can I see it reflected in the text?
AO4 *	Use a range of vocabulary and sentence structures for clarity, purpose and effect, with accurate spelling and punctuation.	• How accurately and clearly do I write? • Are there small errors of grammar, spelling and punctuation I can get rid of?

Look out for the Assessment Objective labels throughout your York Notes Study Guide – these will help to focus your study and revision!

The text used in this Study Guide is the Harper Perennial edition, 2004.

For Anita and Me, AO2 is not examined by Edexcel; AO3 is not examined by Eduqas; and AO4 is not examined by OCR.

HOW TO USE YOUR YORK NOTES STUDY GUIDE

You are probably wondering what is the best and most efficient way to use your York Notes Study Guide on *Anita and Me*. Here are three possibilities:

A **step-by-step** study and revision guide	A **'dip-in' support** when you need it	A **revision guide** after you have finished the text
Step 1: Read Part Two as you read the text, as a companion to help you study it. **Step 2:** When you need to, turn to Parts Three to Five to focus your learning. **Step 3:** Then, when you have finished, use Parts Six and Seven to hone your exam skills, revise and practise for the exam.	Perhaps you know the text quite well, but you want to check your understanding and practise your exam skills? Just look for the section you think you need most help with and go for it!	You might want to use the Notes after you have finished your study, using Parts Two to Five to check over what you have learned, and then work through Parts Six and Seven in the immediate weeks leading up to your exam.

HOW WILL THE GUIDE HELP YOU STUDY AND REVISE?

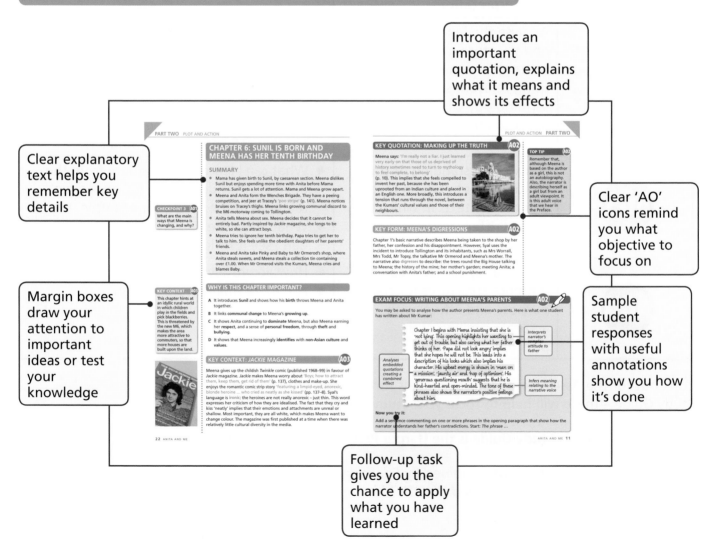

Introduces an important quotation, explains what it means and shows its effects

Clear explanatory text helps you remember key details

Margin boxes draw your attention to important ideas or test your knowledge

Clear 'AO' icons remind you what objective to focus on

Sample student responses with useful annotations show you how it's done

Follow-up task gives you the chance to apply what you have learned

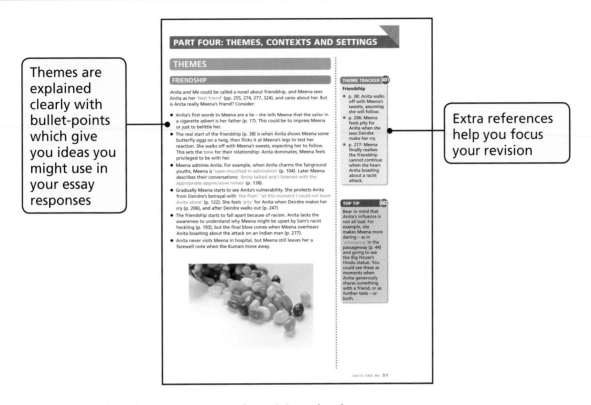

Themes are explained clearly with bullet-points which give you ideas you might use in your essay responses

Extra references help you focus your revision

Parts Two to **Five** end with a **Progress and Revision check**:

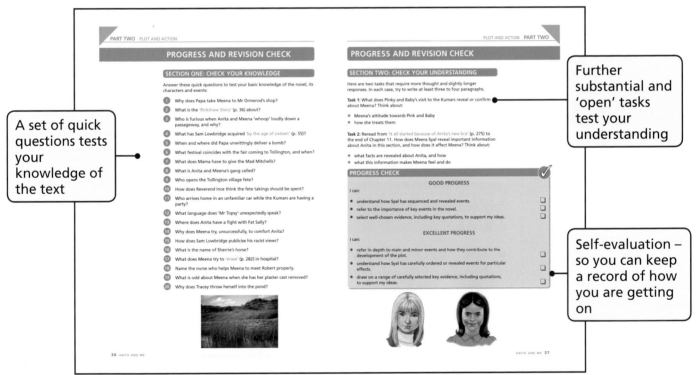

A set of quick questions tests your knowledge of the text

Further substantial and 'open' tasks test your understanding

Self-evaluation – so you can keep a record of how you are getting on

Don't forget **Parts Six** and **Seven**, with advice and practice on **improving your writing skills**:

- Focus on **difficult areas** such as **'context'** and **'inferences'**
- **Short snippets** of **other students' work** to show you how it's done (or not done!)
- Three annotated **sample responses** to a task **at different levels**, with **expert comments**, to help you judge your own level
- **Practice questions**
- **Answers** to the **Progress and Revision Checks** and **Checkpoint** margin boxes

Now it's up to you! Don't forget – there's even more help on our website with more sample answers, essay planners and even online tutorials. Go to **www.yorknotes.com** to find out more.

PART TWO: PLOT AND ACTION

PLOT SUMMARY

PREFACE AND CHAPTERS 1–2: THE TOMBOY LIAR OF TOLLINGTON

- Meena reflects on her earliest memories, presenting and then undercutting a false and clichéd family background.
- Papa takes Meena to Tollington's village shop to find out if she stole money to buy sweets: she eventually confesses.
- Meena describes Tollington, her first encounter with Anita, and a birthday outing when she choked on a sausage.
- We meet the 'Aunties' and 'Uncles'. Meena enjoys their stories of her parents' romance.

CHAPTERS 3–4: MEETING ANITA, THE NEIGHBOURS, AND THE KUMARS AND THEIR FRIENDS

- Local girl Anita Rutter befriends Meena. We hear about the neighbours – Mrs Christmas (who has cancer), Uncle Alan, Hairy Neddy, Sandy, Sam Lowbridge and the Worralls.
- Anita and Meena 'whoop' down a passageway next to the Christmases' house. Later Mrs Christmas dies.
- Papa warns Meena about lying. Meena recalls his musical evenings, and her parents and friends discussing their tragic histories. She learns that Mama is pregnant.

CHAPTER 5: DIWALI, THE FAIR AND A DANGEROUS ADVENTURE

- Anita and Meena go to watch the autumn fair unload. It is the Hindu festival of Diwali and Auntie Shaila tells Meena about Hinduism. Mama drives Meena to a Sikh temple.
- At a family musical gathering, Meena sings a pop song and shocks the adults with a vulgar expression learnt from Anita.
- Anita and Meena visit the fair, Anita telling Meena on the way that a witch lives in the Big House. Anita, Sherrie and Fat Sally pair off with youths working on the fair. Meena protects Anita from learning that Anita's mother, Deirdre, is having sex with Anita's 'boyfriend'.

- Anita leads Meena into the Big House's grounds to see a statue, but they are chased by dogs and Meena loses her mother's diamond necklace. Meena returns to find Mama about to be rushed to hospital.

TOP TIP (A01)

Be clear in your revision and essay writing which parts of the novel are 'present moment' narrative, and which are digressions, when Meena breaks off to recall past incidents or describe neighbours. Also notice how they relate. For example, the story of Meena almost choking on a hot dog (p. 27) is a recollection from two years earlier, but it shows that even then she wanted attention and drama.

CHAPTERS 6–8: SUNIL, THE FETE AND NANIMA'S VISIT

- Meena's brother, Sunil, is born. Meena and Anita form the Wenches Brigade. Meena hears about sex from Anita, and longs to be white, so she can attract boys.
- Following Meena's tenth birthday, she and Anita take Meena's cousins, Pinky and Baby, to the shop, where Anita steals sweets, and Meena steals a collection tin. When found out, Meena blames Baby.
- In the spring, local councillor Mr Pembridge opens the fete, at which Hairy Neddy proposes to Sandy, a fortune-teller warns Meena against Anita, and Meena falls out with Anita over Sam's racist heckling.
- Meena's maternal grandmother, Nanima, arrives from India and helps Mama. Her stories make Meena want to visit India. Meena wrongly accuses Mr Ormerod of cheating Nanima.

CHAPTERS 9–11: MEENA AND ANITA

- Meena and Tracey go to Dale End Farm, with the Rutters' poodle, to see Anita. Anita forgives Meena but goads Fat Sally into a fight. The dog escapes and is hit by a car.
- Anita is upset that Deirdre has walked out, and rebuffs Meena's attempt to comfort her, though she does come to dinner. Mama suspects Anita of stealing her diamond necklace.
- Diggers arrive to bulldoze the village school for the M6. Sam stages a racist publicity stunt. An Indian man is beaten up and robbed. Meena hears that Sam and his gang did it, watched by Anita. Shocked, Meena is thrown from Sherrie's horse and breaks her leg.

CHAPTERS 12–13: CLIMAX AND RESOLUTION

- It is August, and Meena is in hospital. Robert, in an isolation room next to her, gradually becomes her 'boyfriend'.
- Meena comes home at Christmas to find the M6 built and new houses planned. She sees Anita kiss Sam. She writes to Robert, but he has died.
- Meena is more contented, though Sam and Anita's taunting messages distract her from revising. The night before Meena's eleven-plus exam, Tracey arrives, desperate, and leads Meena to Hollow Ponds – where Anita is having sex with Sam.
- Sam kisses Meena, and Anita throws rocks at them. When Sam threatens Anita, Tracey launches herself at him but falls in the pond. Meena runs for help. Tracey is resuscitated. Meena tells the police what happened.
- The Kumars move away, and Meena leaves Anita a farewell note saying she is going to the grammar school.

REVISION FOCUS: RELATIONSHIP TIMELINE

On a timeline, plot the key moments in the development of Meena's relationship with Anita, from first encounter to farewell note. Note the chapter and page of each moment.

TOP TIP (A01)

When revising the plot be aware of its overall development, especially of how developments in Meena's relationship with Anita relate to changes taking place in the village – such as the building of the M6, and even Britain as a whole. Also notice the stages as Meena gradually grows up.

TOP TIP (A01)

If you plan to watch the 2002 film version, do so once you know the novel well. The film contains many of the ingredients of the novel, but merged, altered or reordered. Do not make the mistake of confusing it with the novel.

PREFACE AND CHAPTER 1: INTRODUCTIONS AND A GUILTY CONFESSION

SUMMARY

- The **narrator**, Meena, describes several false **clichéd** 'immigrant' memories. Her first real memory is of understanding a joke. We learn that she has a need to make up stories.
- Nine-year-old Meena has stolen a shilling to buy sweets, claiming that the shopkeeper Mr Ormerod gave them to her. Her father is taking her to check her story.
- Meena describes her village, Tollington, where the mine has shut. The 'Big House' is where its mysterious last owner lives.
- Meena reveals how thrilled she was the first time Anita spoke to her.
- She describes her own mother, and some neighbours.
- Meena worries that her parents will hear about her punishment at school, and admits to lying about the sweets, disappointing her father.

KEY CONTEXT (A03)

Many Indians and Pakistanis moved to Britain in the 1950s and 1960s, but Meena's family is unusual in moving to a village. The fictional village of Tollington is based on Essington, in the West Midlands, where the last coal mine closed in 1968.

WHY IS THIS SECTION IMPORTANT?

A It introduces the **narrator** as a girl who tells **lies**.

B It describes **Tollington** and the context of **mine closure**.

C It introduces Meena's **parents** and her **complicated feelings** for them.

D It introduces **Anita**, whom Meena **admires**.

E Several **local characters** are introduced.

KEY CHARACTERS: MEENA, HER PARENTS AND ANITA (A02)

Meera Syal introduces most of the main characters as part of the **narrative** of nine-year-old Meena being taken to the shop. This incident tells us that she is a child for whom truth is flexible. She has a vivid imagination and needs to make up stories. She lies to get out of trouble, and puts off confessing. However, we also learn that she feels bad about deceiving her father. Her love and respect for him are shown by her affectionate description – his 'sensitive' face and 'generous' mouth, as well as his 'vulnerability and pride' (p. 11). She confesses to save him from the pain of 'public shame' (p. 22). She describes her mother hanging out washing, the language suggesting how important her mother is to her – though she wishes her mother would not dress her like a little girl, and had a more conventional garden.

Anita is identified as a charismatic but unreliable older girl. Her first words to Meena are a lie: she claims a sailor in a cigarette advert is her father. Meena is gratified by the 'radiance' of her smile (p. 17).

KEY QUOTATION: MAKING UP THE TRUTH (A02)

Meena says: 'I'm really not a liar. I just learned very early on that those of us deprived of history sometimes need to turn to mythology to feel complete, to belong'
(p. 10). This implies that she feels compelled to invent her past, because she has been uprooted from an Indian culture and placed in an English one. More broadly, this introduces a tension that runs through the novel, between the Kumars' cultural values and those of their neighbours.

TOP TIP (A02)

Remember that, although Meena is based on the author as a girl, this is not an autobiography. Also, the narrator is describing herself as a girl but from an adult viewpoint. It is this adult voice that we hear in the Preface.

KEY FORM: MEENA'S DIGRESSIONS (A02)

Chapter 1's basic narrative describes Meena being taken to the shop by her father, her confession and his disappointment. However, Syal uses the incident to introduce Tollington and its inhabitants, such as Mrs Worrall, Mrs Todd, Mr Topsy, the talkative Mr Ormerod and Meena's mother. The narrative also digresses to describe: the trees round the Big House talking to Meena; the history of the mine; her mother's garden; meeting Anita; a conversation with Anita's father; and a school punishment.

EXAM FOCUS: WRITING ABOUT MEENA'S PARENTS (A02)

You may be asked to analyse how the author presents Meena's parents. Here is what one student has written about Mr Kumar:

> Chapter 1 begins with Meena insisting that she is 'not lying'. This opening highlights her wanting to get out of trouble, but also caring what her father thinks of her. 'Papa did not look angry' implies that she hopes he will not be. This leads into a description of his looks which also implies his character. His upbeat energy is shown in 'man on a mission', 'jaunty air' and 'hop of optimism'. His 'generous questioning mouth' suggests that he is kind-hearted and open-minded. The tone of these phrases also shows the narrator's positive feelings about him.

Interprets narrator's complex attitude to father

Analyses embedded quotations creating a combined effect

Infers meaning relating to the narrative voice

Now you try it:

Add a sentence commenting on one or more phrases in the opening paragraph that show how the narrator understands her father's contradictions. Start: *The phrase …*

CHECKPOINT 1

What have you learnt so far about how the white English and Indian communities view each other?

KEY CONTEXT **A03**

Meena's father is a Hindu, her mother a Sikh. Both are from the Punjab region that overlaps modern India and Pakistan. There was terrible religious violence there following Partition – the division of British-ruled India into India and Pakistan in 1947. In India, Hindus were in the majority; in Pakistan most of the population was Muslim.

KEY CONTEXT **A03**

'Greek chorus' refers to the chorus in ancient Greek tragedy, a group of actors whose role was to comment on the action of the play.

CHAPTER 2: MAMA AND THE AUNTIES

SUMMARY

- Meena enviously recalls a mad dog. She also recalls a birthday outing when she choked on a sausage and her parents failed to notice.
- Mama is often unhappy about the family's situation. Papa tries to soothe her. When angry she reminds Meena of the goddess Kali; usually she is kind and gracious.
- Mama is angered by Meena's lies and cannot understand why she tells them.
- We meet the 'Aunties' and 'Uncles' – the Kumars' friends. They criticise Meena but shower her with affection. They also criticise the English.
- Meena enjoys tales of her parents' early romance, and stories of Mama's girlhood, especially the 'Rickshaw Story' – about a murder. She craves drama.

WHY IS THIS CHAPTER IMPORTANT?

A It describes Mama's **character** and **background**.

B It reveals Meena's **craving** for **drama** and **attention**.

C It shows us the importance to the **Kumars** of the **Indian community**, and how it differs from the **local** one.

D It shows that Meena is fascinated by **danger and cruelty**, foreshadowing later developments in the novel.

KEY CHARACTERS: MAMA AND THE AUNTIES

Syal presents Mama as a complex and slightly mysterious character. People outside of the family see her 'grace, dignity and unthreatening charm' (p. 28), and the villagers treat her with 'a deferential respect, as if in the company of minor royalty' (p. 28). However, there are other sides to her character. At times she is unhappy – increasingly so: her moods have begun to 'intrude upon every family outing like a fourth silent guest' (p. 25). This foreshadows them featuring in the plot later. Mama is normally calm, but when angry she reminds Meena of the fearsome Hindu goddess Kali. Meena's attitude is also complex: 'I enjoyed her anger ... the glimpse of the monster beneath the mother; it was one of the times I felt we understood each other perfectly' (p. 28). The alliteration of 'monster' and 'mother' underlines the strangeness as they describe the same person.

The Aunties are like deputy mothers. They fulfil 'the role of Greek chorus to mama's epic solo role in my life' (p. 29). Meena resents the friends' interference in her upbringing, but they make her 'feel safe and wanted' (p. 31), and she understands how much they mean to her parents.

KEY LANGUAGE: IMAGERY (A02)

Syal often uses imagery to bring descriptions to life and express Meena's character. For example, Meena chews a sweet 'with the pace and rumination of a sulky cow' (p. 24). This says she is chewing it slowly, but 'sulky' also tells us that she is not really enjoying it – just trying to enjoy what she has 'paid for ... in shame'. The sophisticated nouns tell us that this is the adult narrator criticising her childhood self.

The imagery can provide insights, as in the similes describing how Mama's emotional responses 'would wash across her face like sea changes ... She was as constant as the moon and just as remote' (p. 28). She is reliable ('constant') but emotionally detached. The image of 'the cloud of toddlers that would settle on me like a rash' (p. 25) mixes the metaphor of a cloud of flies with a simile comparing the toddlers to an irritating skin condition.

KEY THEME: CULTURE (A03)

The narrator is caught between cultures. Mama wears a sari to further 'the English people's education' (p. 25), and she scorns English food. Yet she disapproves of Indian women in England wearing garish 'embroidered *salwar kameez* suits' and cheap, 'showy' jewellery (p. 26). Meena, on the other hand, embraces popular English culture, enjoying hot dogs and singing a Disney film song.

Similarly, while Meena sees the family's front garden as 'a social embarrassment' (p. 33), her mother says the English use 'garden frippery' to 'mark out their territory' like dogs. The Aunties respond with a list of English faults, from dirtiness to immorality. This links to the theme of racism: both communities can be prejudiced.

KEY CONTEXT (A03)

Remember that Meena's experience of white English culture is limited to that of a working-class Midlands village, together with what she sees on TV or in films.

AIMING HIGH: COMMENT ON IRONY ⭐

The narrator presents her childhood self with adult understanding, using irony, expressing her own childish viewpoint but making it seem ridiculous. An example is in the imagined tabloid headline, 'TOT CHOKES ON UNCOOKED SAUSAGE! BIRTHDAY RUINED, SAY WEEPING PARENTS!' (p. 37). The adult narrator is ridiculing her own desire for drama. The rhetorical question at the end of the chapter could be seen in the same light. Look for other examples of narrative irony as the novel progresses.

TOP TIP (A02)

Focus on one incident and what it reveals. For example, how do details and language make the 'hot dog' incident (p. 27) melodramatic and ridiculous? How does it express Meena's character?

CHAPTER 3: GETTING TO KNOW ANITA AND OTHER NEIGHBOURS

SUMMARY

- Anita shows Meena some butterfly eggs and walks off with her sweets.
- We hear about Mrs Christmas's cancer, Uncle Alan the Methodist Church youth leader, and the clothes Mrs Christmas donates to his bring-and-buy stall.
- Anita 'whoops' down the passageway next to Mr and Mrs Christmas's house. Meena copies her. Mr Christmas is furious.
- We hear about Hairy Neddy and his band, the Cucumbers, and about Sandy's interest in him.
- Deirdre Rutter considers asking Meena in for tea with Anita, then thinks better of it.
- Meena describes 16-year-old delinquent Sam Lowbridge and his mother Glenys.
- Mrs Worrall teaches Meena to make jam tarts, and introduces her to her disabled husband.

TOP TIP   (A01)

When you have finished reading the novel, go back to find the first mention of each main character, and see how Syal has introduced their role and paved the way for their later development.

WHY IS THIS CHAPTER IMPORTANT?

A It shows Anita starting to get Meena into **trouble**.

B It introduces **local characters** such as Hairy Neddy and Uncle Alan.

C It introduces **Sam Lowbridge**, who is important later in the novel.

D It focuses on **food** as a **cultural feature** and a symbol of **family life**, and shows Meena's lack of interest in **Punjabi cooking**.

E It shows Meena being **sympathetic** to neighbours, such as Mrs Christmas and Mrs Worrall, but less so to her own **mother**.

KEY THEME: FRIENDSHIP

Anita initiates the friendship with Meena by showing her some butterfly eggs on a privet leaf, then flicking the twig at Meena's legs to see if she will flinch. Anita shows her dominance by walking off with Meena's sweets, expecting Meena to follow. Meena does, feeling 'privileged to be in her company' (p. 38). Anita encourages her to run down the echoing passageway next to the Christmases' house 'whooping like an ambulance siren' (p. 44). However, we see a contrast between them when Mr Christmas is angry: Meena apologises but Anita is rude to him. Meena meets Anita's younger, badly treated sister Tracey, and expects to be asked in for tea. Mrs Rutter seems to disapprove of Meena, but Anita still wants to see her the next day.

KEY CHARACTERS: LOCAL CHARACTERS

The novel creates a sense of community by making events in the present trigger Meena's memories of local characters. For example, when Anita approaches the Christmases' house, this makes Meena think of Mrs Christmas, whose terminal cancer is discussed in whispers by the local women. This in turn makes her describe Uncle Alan, because Mrs Christmas donated clothes to his bring-and-buy sale. His friendly enthusiasm pulls children into his fund-raising and community schemes, while to younger women he is 'the nearest thing we had to a sex symbol' (p. 41).

Hairy Neddy is a comic character who drives a three-wheeler van for his entertainment business: he plays an electric organ. Despite being a 'plump, piggy-eyed' man with too much hair (p. 47), he is the object of sexual innuendo from local women, and Sandy the divorcee hopes to attract him.

Mrs Worrall is presented more seriously. She is fond of Meena and teaches her to make pastry. She cares for her war-casualty husband, yet is rarely visited by their grown-up children. This highlights a cultural difference between the white English and the more closely knit Indian families.

> **CHECKPOINT 2** **A01**
>
> What have you learnt about the budding friendship between Meena and Anita so far?

> **TOP TIP** **A02**
>
> Look for clues to Deirdre Rutter's character in her physical appearance (see p. 55).

REVISION FOCUS: THE PRESENT MOMENT AND DIGRESSIONS

- Make a three-column table. Head column 1 'Present moment', column 2 'Digression' and column 3 'What it shows'.
- In column 1 note what happens in the 'present moment' narrative in Chapter 3 – such as Anita showing Meena the butterfly eggs.
- In column 2, on the row beneath each present moment event, note what characters and events Meena describes when she digresses, such as her collecting for Uncle Alan.
- Use column 3 to note how these events and digressions describe Meena.

CHAPTER 4: INDIAN HERITAGE AND FAMILY VALUES

SUMMARY

- Papa warns Meena about lying. To show he forgives her, he agrees to tell her a story from his life in India.
- Meena recalls her father's musical evenings, and how her parents and friends once discussed their experiences of religious violence.
- Papa relates how, as a teenager, he unknowingly delivered a bomb to a Muslim's house.
- The neighbours gather to see Mrs Christmas's body being taken away. Meena worries that she and Anita killed her by 'whooping'. Mama attends the funeral.
- We learn how Mama manages Papa's moods. Meena compares their relationship with those of friends and neighbours.
- Meena is not pleased to hear that Mama is going to have a baby.

WHY IS THIS CHAPTER IMPORTANT?

A It reveals more of Meena's **relationship** with her **father**.

B It describes how the **Indian community** preserve their **culture**.

C We find out more about the **Partition violence** that is part of Indian history.

D Mr Christmas has been able to **conceal his wife's death** suggesting to the Kumars that **English families** are **less close-knit than Indian ones**.

E We learn more about **Mama and Papa's relationship**.

KEY THEME: TRUTH AND FICTION   (A02)

KEY CONTEXT (A03)

Opportunity Knocks was an early talent show, a precursor of shows like *X-Factor*. It began on radio, but its main TV run was from 1964 to 1978, when it was hosted by Hughie Green.

This is the evening of the day when Meena lies about stealing, as described in Chapter 1. Her father tells her the story of 'the boy and the tiger' to show her that 'if you tell lies too often, no one will believe you when you are telling the truth' (p. 70). When Meena recognises it as a version of the English 'Boy who cried wolf' story, she drifts into a fantasy about being on *Opportunity Knocks*. But the truth of the story is apparent when she tells Mama that she saw Mrs Christmas earlier, but is told that she has 'done enough lying for one day' (p. 78). Meena is only interested in the truth if it is exciting, as in Papa's bomb story.

KEY QUOTATION: HISTORY (A03)

Meena says that for her parents the past is 'a murky bottomless pool full of monsters and the odd shining coin, with a deceptively still surface and a deadly undercurrent' (p. 75). The Kumars and their friends share memories of the religious violence which uprooted them from their homes and is partly why they emigrated. The pool **metaphor** implies that ordinary people behaved like 'monsters' and that emotions linked to the past could still have a powerful, even 'deadly' effect.

EXAM FOCUS: WRITING ABOUT CULTURAL DIFFERENCES (A03)

You may be asked to write about how the author presents cultural differences. Here is what one student has written about this theme:

> Indian culture is represented by Papa's musical evenings, when he sings folk songs and recites love poetry. The Aunties and Uncles visit and form a kind of extended family. They all know about each other's lives and Indian histories. White English culture, on the other hand, is represented by the women drunkenly 'piling off' the bus from the Flamingo Night Club: this phrase makes them seem uncivilised by comparison with the Aunties.
>
> Also, while family connections are important to the Kumars and their friends – they worry about their parents in India – the Christmases' children rarely visit though they live nearby. This is why Mrs Christmas has been 'dead for weeks' before anyone finds out.

Clear topic sentence

Clearly signals a comparison

Explains textual evidence

Complex sentence using 'while', to compare

Now you try it:

Add a sentence commenting on how cultural difference is explored when Mama decides to attend the Christmases' funeral (p. 79). Start: *Mama attended …*

KEY CHARACTERS: MAMA AND PAPA (A02)

In Chapter 2, Papa managed Mama's moods; Chapter 4 shows Mama speaking to Papa in 'soothing but firm' tones when the metaphorical 'big black crow' of depression settles on him (p. 80). Meena compares her mother's handling of him to the men running fairground rides – an **image** which anticipates the fair described in Chapter 5. As in Chapter 2, Meena is fascinated by her parents' youthful romance, and notices that they still appreciate each other: 'I presumed that this was what love meant, both people thinking they were the lucky one' (p. 82). Unlike other adult couples, they have 'managed to retain ... an openness, a flirty banter', by which she is 'both fascinated and embarrassed' (p. 83).

KEY CONTEXT (A03)

The *ghazal* that Papa performs is a poem consisting of rhyming couplets with a refrain. It may deal with romantic or religious love. The form originated in the Arabic-speaking Middle East, but spread to northern India.

CHAPTER 5, PART 1: THE FAIR ARRIVES AT DIWALI (pp. 88–106)

SUMMARY

- It is late October. Anita's family now has a poodle. Mama is shocked by its racist name but Papa is amused.
- Anita and Meena go to see the fair unload.
- It is the Hindu festival of Diwali, and Auntie Shaila tells Meena about Hindu belief in reincarnation, making Meena anxious.
- Mama takes Meena to the Sikh *gurudwara* (temple) to learn about Sikhism. It is Mama's first solo driving trip, and the car rolls back at the lights: Meena has to ask drivers to reverse.
- Anita and Meena go to the fair, Anita telling Meena on the way that a witch lives in the Big House. We hear about Jodie Bagshot, who drowned in Hollow Ponds.
- Anita, Sherrie and Fat Sally pair off with three youths working at the fair, excluding Meena.

WHY IS THIS SECTION IMPORTANT?

A It gives evidence of **racism** – both **casual** and more **deliberate**.

B Meena learns more about her **religious heritage** – both **Hindu** and **Sikh** – and therefore worries about the consequences of her **lying**.

C It shows that Mama has **weaknesses**.

D The **relationship** between Meena and Anita develops, though we see Anita's **selfish** readiness to **exclude** Meena when it suits her.

E Meena is beginning to learn about **sex** and **courtship**.

TOP TIP **(A02)**

Look out for language revealing the adult narrator's often ironic assessment of her nine-year-old self, as in 'I nodded wisely. Of course, I had known this all along' (p. 106).

TOP TIP: WRITING ABOUT RACISM   **(A01)**

Show that you understand the different levels of racism in the novel, and how far racism is the result of ignorance or real malice. For example, Deirdre may name the family poodle as she does just because she thinks this is appropriate for a black dog, or there may be more deliberate racism at work. Notice how Syal shows the different possible interpretations in Mama and Papa's responses. Mama is appalled, but Papa laughs at what he assumes is the simple ignorance of people like Deirdre (p. 90).

A clearer example is when Meena has to ask drivers to reverse. An elderly woman responds with a stream of racist abuse (p. 97). You might comment on how Syal criticises racism here: she uses the woman's poor vocabulary to imply her limited intelligence.

KEY THEME: GROWING UP   **(A02)**

Meena is still a child. For example, she believes Anita's claim that a witch lives in the Big House. Yet she is already dimly aware of sex. She observes Anita, Sherrie and Fat Sally trying to attract three youths who work at the fair. She notices, but cannot yet understand, Anita's ability to charm them: 'I stood open-mouthed in admiration, wondering what spell she had cast, to turn these boy-men ... into grinning, pliant pets' (p. 104). As Meena watches the courtship 'ritual', with the girls huddling together and the boys sitting 'with their legs as wide as possible', she is 'beginning to realise' that this resembles the mating behaviour of dogs (p. 105). Later, she feigns understanding when Anita asks if she is still a virgin (p. 248). This will get her into trouble with Papa when she repeats the question at home.

KEY CONTEXT: INDIAN RELIGIONS   **(A03)**

It is Diwali, the Hindu Festival of Lights, which Mama tells Mrs Worrall is 'Our Christmas' (p. 91). This celebrates the victory of light over darkness, and good over evil. Meena wishes her family had a shrine to honour the gods, like Auntie Shaila's. Shaila tells her about reincarnation, the belief that individuals are reborn after death, their new life form and situation depending on the positive or negative energy (*karma*) that their deeds have generated. Mama and Papa also celebrate Christmas, Mama (a Sikh) calling this 'a typical example of Hindu tolerance' for other faiths (p. 92).

TOP TIP   **(A02)**

Notice how Syal uses Meena's limited knowledge to arouse our curiosity by withholding information. An example is her observation that Deirdre seems 'very busy for a woman who claimed not to have a job' and comes home 'bustling with secrets' (p. 90).

KEY CONTEXT   **(A03)**

Like the Christian festival of Easter, Diwali's timing depends on the phases of the moon, so it can fall between mid-October and mid-November.

CHAPTER 5, PART 2: DANGEROUS ADVENTURES (pp. 106–30)

SUMMARY

- Mama prepares for a musical gathering, despite being heavily pregnant. Meena puts on Mama's make-up and diamond necklace, but is told to remove the make-up.
- Papa sings to the Aunties and Uncles, but Meena is reluctant. She reflects bitterly on the Indian custom of polite refusal, and recalls Mama having to give the Mad Mitchells a lift because they accepted her offer.
- Everyone applauds when Meena sings a pop song – until she shocks them with an expression learnt from Anita. Later she overhears Mama listing her misdemeanours.
- Meena slips out to the fair, where Sam Lowbridge helps her win a bracelet. She bumps into Sherrie, then goes on rides with Anita, protecting her from discovering that Deirdre is probably having sex with Anita's 'boyfriend'.
- Anita leads Meena into the Big House's grounds to see a Hindu statue. They are pursued by dogs, Meena losing Mama's necklace and cutting her face. She returns to find Mama about to be rushed to hospital.

WHY IS THIS SECTION IMPORTANT?

A It shows that Meena wants to **grow up**, and prefers **English culture** and **customs** to **Indian** ones.

B Sam Lowbridge is **kind** to Meena.

C It introduces **Hollow Ponds**, which feature in the novel's climax.

D Meena and Anita's **relationship strengthens**. Meena is influenced by Anita but protects her. The pair **bond** through **shared adventure**.

E The chapter ends on a cliffhanger. Will Mama and the baby **survive**?

KEY THEME: FRIENDSHIP

Meena and Anita's friendship is like a rollercoaster. Earlier in the chapter Anita ignored Meena to flirt with 'the Poet' (p. 104); now Anita enjoys fairground rides with Meena, perhaps because no one else is available. Meena shows loyalty and compassion when she stays with Anita to keep her from discovering that she is being betrayed by her own mother.

The friendship deepens when they share the adventure in the Big House grounds. Anita is showing that she rates Meena highly enough to take her to see her secret, the statue, and Meena shows her bravery, especially when she goes right up to the statue. The girls bond further when they share the danger of being pursued by dogs.

KEY THEME: CULTURE (A03)

For Diwali, Mama and Papa host another musical gathering. Meena starts by wearing a traditional *salwar kameez* suit, but later changes into English clothes, in which she feels more herself. Papa is inspired by his own performance to ask her to sing. She begins a Hindi film song that he has taught her, but when she hears Shaila comment on her Birmingham accent, she stops. When Papa says, 'You should sing your own songs, Meena' (p. 114) he is referring to her Indian heritage, but Meena takes it to mean the pop songs that she prefers. The guests are open-minded enough to enjoy her singing 'We Wear Short Shorts', but a culture clash occurs when she misuses an obscene phrase to praise the song (p. 115). The moment itself is dramatically important and relates to the themes of culture and growing up, and to Meena's relationship with Anita and her parents, and the Aunties and Uncles.

KEY CHARACTER: SAM LOWBRIDGE (A02)

We see more of Sam Lowbridge when he gently guides Meena to win a prize on the shooting range. However, his ambiguous character is implied by the target she hits: a racist representation of a black man.

AIMING HIGH: COMMENT ON STRUCTURE ⭐

To write about structure, 'stand back' to see how the text develops. Here, the tension mounts to an explosive climax. First, Meena behaves badly in several ways. She takes Mama's necklace and puts on make-up. Then she unintentionally shocks the adults by misusing language learnt from Anita. We know she feels confused and threatened by their disapproval from her 'sense of overwhelming menace' (p. 115). This prepares us for her reaction when she hears Mama listing her 'misdemeanours' (p. 117): she risks greater disapproval by sneaking off to the fair.

The sense of Meena entering forbidden territory is heightened by sexual references – Sherrie's love bite (p. 120) and Deirdre and 'the Poet', with 'hands tugging at each other's buttons' (p. 121). It grows when Anita leads Meena into the woods: 'a syrupy gloom which somewhere housed a child-eating monster' (p. 124). They pass Hollow Ponds, dangerous at night, and spy into the Big House. The mystery of the marble statue gives way to mounting tension and quickening pace as they are pursued by dogs and Meena loses Mama's necklace and gashes her face. Syal makes us anticipate Meena getting into terrible trouble, but the real climax is the surprise cliffhanger of the threat to Mama and the baby.

KEY CONTEXT (A03)

Jackie (p. 126) was a popular magazine published from 1964 to 1993. It was aimed at young teenage girls but was often read by pre-teens too.

KEY CONTEXT (A03)

The statue in the Big House grounds is of the elephant-headed Ganesha, a widely worshipped Hindu god associated with success, wisdom and the arts.

CHAPTER 6: SUNIL IS BORN AND MEENA HAS HER TENTH BIRTHDAY

SUMMARY

- Mama has given birth to Sunil, by caesarean section. Meena dislikes Sunil but enjoys spending more time with Anita before Mama returns. Sunil gets a lot of attention. Mama and Meena grow apart.

- Meena and Anita form the Wenches Brigade. They have a peeing competition, and jeer at Tracey's 'poo stripe' (p. 141). Meena notices bruises on Tracey's thighs. Meena links growing communal discord to the M6 motorway coming to Tollington.

- Anita tells Meena about sex. Meena decides that it cannot be entirely bad. Partly inspired by *Jackie* magazine, she longs to be white, so she can attract boys.

- Meena tries to ignore her tenth birthday. Papa tries to get her to talk to him. She feels unlike the obedient daughters of her parents' friends.

- Meena and Anita take Pinky and Baby to Mr Ormerod's shop, where Anita steals sweets, and Meena steals a collection tin containing over £1.00. When Mr Ormerod visits the Kumars, Meena cries and blames Baby.

> **CHECKPOINT 3** (A01)
>
> What are the main ways that Meena is changing, and why?

WHY IS THIS CHAPTER IMPORTANT?

A It introduces **Sunil** and shows how his **birth** throws Meena and Anita together.

B It links **communal change** to Meena's **growing up**.

C It shows Anita continuing to **dominate** Meena, but also Meena earning her **respect**, and a sense of **personal freedom**, through **theft** and **bullying**.

D It shows that Meena increasingly **identifies** with **non-Asian culture** and **values**.

> **KEY CONTEXT** (A03)
>
> This chapter hints at an idyllic rural world in which children play in the fields and pick blackberries. This is threatened by the new M6, which makes the area more attractive to commuters, so that more houses are built upon the land.

KEY CONTEXT: *JACKIE* MAGAZINE (A03)

Meena gives up the childish *Twinkle* comic (published 1968–99) in favour of *Jackie* magazine. *Jackie* makes Meena worry about 'Boys; how to attract them, keep them, get rid of them' (p. 137), clothes and make-up. She enjoys the romantic comic strip story 'featuring a limpid-eyed, anorexic, blonde heroine ... who cried as neatly as she kissed' (pp. 137–8). Syal's language is **ironic**: the heroines are not really anorexic – just thin. This word expresses her criticism of how they are idealised. The fact that they cry and kiss 'neatly' implies that their emotions and attachments are unreal or shallow. Most important, they are all white, which makes Meena want to change colour. The magazine was first published at a time when there was relatively little cultural diversity in the media.

KEY CHARACTER: MEENA THE MISFIT (A02)

Meena feels she is a misfit, and Sunil's birth helps to distance her from her parents. With Mama in hospital, Meena is 'temporarily motherless and a proven liar and thief' (p. 133). Since Fat Sally's mother has stopped her going out with Anita, Anita is officially 'a Bad Influence', so Meena concludes that her friendship with Anita is 'a marriage made in heaven' (p. 133).

The obvious way in which Meena is a misfit in her Midlands village is her Asian background. Hence she writes to *Jackie*: 'I am brown, although I do not wear thick glasses. Will this stop me getting a guy?' (p. 145). The magazine's advice, to try to cover up with make-up, hardly helps her to accept her ethnicity. She wants to 'emerge, pink and unrecognisable' (p. 146). She is beginning to ignore reprimands. She explains: 'I knew I was a freak of some kind, too mouthy, clumsy and scabby to be a real Indian girl, too Indian to be a real Tollington wench' (pp. 149–50). However, she is accepted by Anita, especially when she steals, lies and bullies Pinky and Baby.

TOP TIP (A02)

Look out for implied information. The 'row of bruises around Tracey's thighs ... mimicking the imprint of ten cruel, angry fingers' (p. 142) implies that Tracey is being abused; Meena saying she wished she had not seen this implies that she does not want to get involved. However, it may be only the adult **narrator** who interprets the bruises.

EXAM FOCUS: WRITING ABOUT HOW MEENA CHANGES (A01)

Here is what one student has written about how Meena changes:

> Earlier in the novel Meena has been presented as a caring girl. For example, In Chapter 1 she confesses to stealing because she does not want Papa to be shamed in Mr Ormerod's shop. However, in Chapter 6 we see two stages of her changing. First, in the peeing competition, when Tracey is taunted for having a 'poo stripe', and Meena remains passive: 'I did not join in, neither did I help her disentangle herself. I merely watched'. However, later in the chapter she is more seriously dishonest, and actively cruel and bullying, when she steals a charity collection tin and hides it in Baby's jumper, frightening her into silence with a threat.

Example illustrates the point

Well chosen quotation gives evidence of the first stage

Language points to comparison, showing development

Now you try it:

Add a sentence commenting on Meena's behaviour when Mr Ormerod comes to the Kumars' house. Start: *When Mr Ormerod visits …*

CHAPTER 7: THE SPRING FETE

SUMMARY

- The Tollington women are doing their spring cleaning.
- Meena comments on how the Swinging Sixties bypassed Tollington, on widespread racism, and on Miss India becoming Miss World.
- Meena wants Sunil to be given to an orphanage. Mama seems exhausted. She and Papa discuss racism.
- Mr Pembridge opens the village fete, held in his grounds. He claims to oppose the M6. Hairy Neddy helps to make Sandy's stall a success, and proposes to her. We hear that the Tollington women try to flirt with Papa, and that he enjoys gambling.
- Meena and Anita have their fortunes told, and Anita leaves furious. The fortune-teller warns Meena against Anita. Meena describes Anita's forceful personality.
- Reverend Ince announces that the fete's takings will buy a new chapel roof. Sam Lowbridge objects, and Uncle Alan sympathises with him. When Sam's heckling becomes racist, Meena is shocked, then angry with Anita for admiring him.
- With Mama on the verge of a breakdown, Meena hears that Nanima is going to visit.

KEY CONTEXT **A03**

Reita Faria (Rita Farrier), already Miss India, became Miss World in 1966. She went on to become a doctor, marrying another doctor, David Powell, and moving to Dublin.

WHY IS THIS CHAPTER IMPORTANT?

A It links the **threat to village traditions** with Meena feeling **insecure** about **change**.

B It describes various forms of **racism**, **climaxing** in Sam Lowbridge's **outburst**.

C We see how **difficult** Mama is finding life, which leads to Nanima's visit.

D Meena and Anita **fall out** for the first time, as **foreshadowed** by the **fortune-teller**.

KEY THEME: RACISM

Meena comments on how rare it is to see someone from an ethnic minority on TV, especially in a positive role. She feels as if her home is 'another planet' (p. 165) because Asian culture seems invisible in England. She recalls her parents discussing racist employers, although they acknowledge that 'some of these [English] people are angels' (p. 166). They discuss the patronising racism of Mr Ormerod, and neighbours who accept them only because 'they don't think we are really Indian' (p. 172). Hearing about racist attacks, Meena feels 'both impotent and on fire' (p. 173). This prepares us for her shock at Sam's outburst against giving charity to 'darkies we've never met' (p. 193). Meena is angry with Anita because Anita is too insensitive to see that she might be upset (p. 195).

KEY CONTEXT (A03)

The 'Swinging Sixties' are often seen as the time when the contraceptive pill made accidental pregnancy less likely, when some young people began to use drugs, and when the pop music scene took off – with bands like the Beatles and the Rolling Stones. Both performed on *Ready Steady Go!* (p. 164), a TV music programme which ran from 1963 to 1966.

REVISION FOCUS: COMIC EXAGGERATION

Find and learn some examples of Syal's comic exaggeration, and be prepared to analyse their effect. For example, she describes the Mad Mitchells' rubbish forming a 'bizarre monument to kitsch' (p. 163), as if they are commemorating an art form. She says that for most of the year the Pembridge mansion 'remained out of bounds to us, as effectively as if it had been surrounded by electric fences and a shark-infested moat' (p. 167). This

implies that, although the Pembridges host the fete, they actually fear and loath the villagers. Their son is ridiculed as sitting on a horse as if he is 'waiting for it to explode underneath him' (p. 168). What other examples can you find?

CHECKPOINT 4 (A01)

What indications of personal and social change are there in the spring fete episode?

KEY THEME: CHANGE (A02)

The chapter contrasts the tradition of the fete, and the Pembridges' Tudor mansion, unchanged for centuries, with the threat of change. Positive change is represented by spring cleaning. Racism, however, is a threatening change of which Meena becomes increasingly aware. Syal foreshadows this by commenting on how 'the familiar could turn into the unknown' (p. 173). We also see

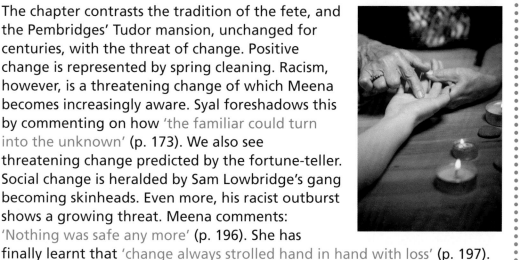

threatening change predicted by the fortune-teller. Social change is heralded by Sam Lowbridge's gang becoming skinheads. Even more, his racist outburst shows a growing threat. Meena comments: 'Nothing was safe any more' (p. 196). She has finally learnt that 'change always strolled hand in hand with loss' (p. 197). The casual personification makes the idea seem all the more sinister.

TOP TIP (A02)

Look for signs that Meena is gradually embracing her Indian cultural heritage as well as the Western one, as when she identifies with the Hindu goddess as well as Superman, and when she resents Mr Topsy knowing more Punjabi than her.

CHAPTER 8: NANIMA'S VISIT

SUMMARY

- Mama's mother, Nanima, arrives from India. Meena immediately likes her. The welcome party attracts friendly attention from neighbours and a mystery figure from the Big House.
- Thanks to Nanima, Sunil sleeps better and becomes less dependent on Mama, and more attached to Meena, who now helps to look after him.
- Nanima's dramatic stories make Meena want to visit India. They contradict the British version of history that makes Meena ashamed in school. One story leads to education being discussed. Meena feels under pressure to pass her eleven-plus exam.
- Deirdre thinks Mama has stopped Meena from seeing Anita. Mama reassures her.
- Nanima meets some neighbours, and talks in Punjabi with 'Mr Topsy'. Meena invents a colourful background for her.
- Meena sends Nanima into Mr Ormerod's shop, then accuses him of cheating Nanima.
- Meena shows she is still furious with Sam, but then becomes ill. Nanima tells the story of her life in British-ruled India.

CHECKPOINT 5 (A01)

In what ways is Nanima's visit important for Meena?

WHY IS THIS CHAPTER IMPORTANT?

A It shows the importance of **family**, and how Nanima helps Meena feel **less alienated**.

B It raises the issues of **colonialism**, **biased history** and **cultural integration**.

C It develops two **mysteries**: the **Big House**, and Deirdre's possible **affair**.

D It shows Meena's growing **anger** about **racism**.

KEY CHARACTER: NANIMA

Nanima rapidly becomes a major influence in Meena's life. She seems to have a magical effect on the Kumar family, relieving the strain on Mama and encouraging Sunil's development, reflected in the passage when Meena dreams that Nanima is flying like a god (p. 207). Although she speaks little English, she and Meena seem to understand each other, sometimes through 'a language called Grunt' (p. 217) rather than speech, although Meena makes an effort to learn Punjabi. Nanima is motherly towards Meena, whom she affectionately calls a 'junglee' (p. 200), implying that she approves of Meena's wild and rebellious side. Nanima is an independent woman, taking the initiative to visit the Worralls, and going into Mr Ormerod's shop despite not speaking English. Her stories about her life in India give Meena a sense of belonging, a cultural context and an alternative view of Indian history.

KEY CHARACTER: MEENA

Nanima's visit is part of Meena's growing up. Perhaps it is surprising that she accepts Nanima sleeping in her bed with her, but this shows that she appreciates Nanima's motherly protection. She in turn feels protective towards Nanima, as shown when she challenges Mr Ormerod about Nanima's change. Meena seems to be discovering a new power in herself, coupled with self-control: when she dismisses Sam Lowbridge, she says, 'I felt sharp and bright as a knife. I cut carefully' (p. 227). When she silences his gang with her glare, she identifies both with Superman and a many-armed Hindu goddess. At the same time, she wants to see Anita because she is moved by the sight of her crying.

AIMING HIGH: COMMENT ON FORESHADOWING

Syal uses **foreshadowing** to stimulate our curiosity and make later events, when they occur, seem satisfyingly inevitable. Here, we see Deirdre arrive home in an 'unfamiliar car'. Syal creates a mood of mystery by revealing information gradually: 'I saw a hennaed beehive briefly collide with a blonde male head' (p. 205). Only in the next sentence do we find that the beehive hairdo is Deirdre's. Our probable suspicion that the 'collision' is a goodnight kiss is confirmed by the mood of her 'jaunty walk' (p. 206) and her need to 'fiddle' with her bra strap. These hints add to others, such as her being 'bustling with secrets' (p. 90).

Another example of foreshadowing is the 'figure, huge and shaggy as a bear' (p. 206) watching the party. The **metaphor** of the 'veil of waving bushes' partly concealing the torch adds to the sense of mystery. Another clue is that the torch seems to 'throb' (p. 206) in time with the Indian song, implying that its owner knows the song.

KEY CONTEXT A03

The goddess in Auntie Shaila's shrine (p. 228) may be Durga, the Hindu mother goddess **symbolising** power, morality and protection. In another form she is known as Kali, who is associated with destruction. Her many arms symbolise her great power and her ability to do many things at once.

KEY QUOTATION: IMAGERY A02

Meena describes her momentary impression of Sam and his gang as 'a cluster of shaven heads, downy and vulnerable as dandelion clocks, peeking out at me from the hollyhocks and yarrow stalks' (p. 226). At this point she is becoming ill, although we discover that she has a 'very high temperature' only on page 229. Her fever influences her perception, but it may give her insights rather than just clouding her judgement. Sam and his gang, like other 'skinheads', have 'shaven heads' because they want to look tough, but the **simile** comparing them to 'dandelion clocks', together with the descriptive adjectives, makes them seem just the opposite. The verb 'peeking' makes them seem like shy fairies among the flowers, not thugs.

CHAPTERS 9 AND 10: ANITA AND FAT SALLY FIGHT

SUMMARY

- Meena calls on Anita. Finding she is at Dale End Farm with Sherrie, Meena invites Tracey to accompany her there. They take the poodle.
- We learn that Sherrie's family are moving away because the M6 is being built next to their home.
- Anita forgives Meena. She uses Fat Sally's scarf to secure the poodle, then goads Fat Sally into a fight, and digs her fingernails into Fat Sally's face. The dog breaks free and runs off. Unconcerned, Anita rides Sherrie's pony.
- The poodle is hit by a red car, probably Graham Pembridge's Porsche (see p. 168). Hairy Neddy stops Anita from hitting the dog with a rock to put it out of its misery. Meena reflects that she resented the dog unfairly because of its name, which it could not choose.
- Anita is upset because Deirdre has left. Meena tries to comfort her but is rebuffed. Anita asks her if she is a virgin. Later, Papa is angry when Meena asks if she is. When Meena reveals that Deirdre has left, Mama invites Anita to dinner.
- Anita comes and eats fish fingers – rejecting Indian food. Afterwards, she and Meena try on Meena's clothes. Anita tries to leave with some of them, but Mama stops her.

CHECKPOINT 6 (A01)

What hints and events throughout the novel have led up to Deirdre's departure?

WHY ARE THESE CHAPTERS IMPORTANT?

A We see Anita being **manipulative, violent** and **fearless**, but also **vulnerable** and **ignorant**.

B Meena is reinstated as Anita's **friend**, but still gets Meena into **trouble**.

C Deirdre **exits** Anita's life, and the novel, leading Mama and Papa to **highlight cultural differences** in their different **responses**.

D **Food** is again used to show **cultural differences** and **prejudices**.

KEY CONTEXT (A03)

Biba (p. 241) was a London fashion store in business from 1964 to 1975.

KEY CHARACTER: ANITA (A02)

Anita is masterfully manipulative when she provokes Fat Sally into physically attacking her. She uses Sally's expensive Biba scarf to tie up the poodle, then, when Sally objects, uses this as an excuse to insult her and her family for being 'rich', and to say that Sally will be attending a school for 'posh' girls (p. 239). In the fight, Anita remains coolly self-controlled, simply digging her nails into Fat Sally's face, knowing that this will eventually force her to back off. She shows a similar detachment and determination when she is prepared to kill the dying poodle with a rock (p. 244).

KEY LANGUAGE: VIOLENCE AND DRAMA (A02)

Syal introduces the fight with a **subordinate clause** that builds up our anticipation: 'Before anyone knew what was happening' (p. 240). Her language creates a sense of rapid action. Fat Sally gives 'a strangled scream, grabbing handfuls of hair' (p. 240), conveying her fury. The violent confusion is shown by 'the tangle of kicking, biting, scratching bodies'. This is contrasted with Anita's eerie calm: 'She did not utter one word, emit one moan, her breathing was steady' (p. 241). The fight ends with the poodle escaping, Syal heightening the drama by using 'screamed' on three consecutive lines for Tracey, Sherrie and Fat Sally.

KEY CONTEXT (A03)

Anita arrives for dinner 'empty-handed' (p. 252), whereas Indian guests would bring gifts or contributions. When eating, she makes 'a fortress of her arms' (p. 253). The **metaphor** implies that she feels a need to guard her food.

EXAM FOCUS: WRITING ABOUT MEENA'S RELATIONSHIP WITH ANITA (A01)

You may be asked to analyse how the author presents Meena's relationship with Anita. Here is what one student has written about it:

> Anita enjoys power: even when forgiving Meena, she relishes her 'amazement'. Yet, rather than feeling controlled, Meena feels 'light-headed and free' to be with Anita again. More surprisingly, it is when she has seen Anita at her worst, after the fight, that Meena suddenly pities her: 'Sorrow flooded me ... She needed me maybe more than I needed her.' However, she still finds Anita unpredictable. For example, when she tries to comfort her, Anita violently pushes her away, seeming to hate the suggestion that she is weak enough to need comfort.

Develops the argument, using a connective and an embedded quotation

Shows the changing relationship in context, with a key quotation

Offers an interpretation based on textual evidence

Now you try it:

Add a sentence or two commenting on Anita asking Meena if she is a virgin (p. 248) and its consequences. Start: *Anita demonstrates ...*

TOP TIP: WRITING ABOUT CONTRADICTIONS (A02)

Consider the contradictions in Anita's character. For example, she praises Meena's clothes, but then tries to smuggle ten suits out of the house, along with other things belonging to Meena.

CHAPTER 11: THE DIGGERS ARRIVE

SUMMARY

- Papa has been promoted. Meena recalls biting a girl, and receiving a disappointing present, at one of his office Christmas parties.

- Sunil is learning to talk. Nanima ties a thread to his wrist to ward off evil. Anita seems unchanged, but Tracey is increasingly insecure.

- Mama discovers her diamond necklace has gone. She suspects Anita, but dismisses this thought. There is talk of Enoch Powell, and of families being sent back to India.

- Diggers arrive to bulldoze the village school for the M6. Meena notices an Indian man with the workers. Sam Lowbridge uses the TV news presence to stage a racist publicity stunt. The Indian man (Rajesh Bhatra) is later found beaten up and robbed.

- Anita and Sherrie discuss bras. When Meena overhears Anita telling Sherrie how much she enjoyed watching Sam's gang beat up the Indian man, she decides to ride Trixie.

- Meena is thrown from the horse and breaks her leg. Her parents arrive.

KEY CONTEXT A03

In 1968 the Conservative MP Enoch Powell made a controversial speech in the West Midlands predicting that immigration would lead to huge social problems. It came to be known as the 'Rivers of Blood' speech because of a line from a Roman poet that it quoted. Powell was dismissed from the Shadow Cabinet the next day because of the speech.

WHY IS THIS CHAPTER IMPORTANT?

A **Change** arrives in many forms, from Sunil talking, to the building of the **M6** and growing **racism**.

B Sam Lowbridge shows **energy and daring**, but uses them misguidedly.

C It shows an **Indian man** in a **professional role**, but who is also the **victim of a racist attack**.

D Its climax makes Meena see that she and Anita **cannot be real friends**.

E It develops the **diamond necklace** storyline, which will reappear later.

KEY STRUCTURE: BUILDING TO A CLIMAX (A02)

The opening paragraph **foreshadows** events to come, telling us that this will be a momentous chapter for Meena's childhood. In writing 'If I had known what was going to happen' (p. 259), Syal's **narrator** is looking back from a *present* narrative moment, to a point in the imagined *future* of the narrated *past*! She adds to the sense of foreboding by referring back to 'the Mysterious Stranger' of Chapter 7 (p. 184), and telling us how she would have behaved had she known.

After this, we are lulled into a false sense of security by Papa's promotion, and a touching picture of Sunil learning to speak, before, as Meena puts it, everything starts 'falling apart' (p. 266). First Mama finds that her necklace is missing; then the diggers arrive, bringing massive disruption, and leading indirectly to Sam Lowbridge's racist TV publicity stunt, and his gang's attack on the Indian man. Social change in the form of the M6 and racism becomes part of Meena's growing up, building up to her personal crisis. It is almost as if she breaks her leg in order to achieve the unavoidable emotional break from her friend.

REVISION FOCUS: SEEING PLOT CONNECTIONS

Make a spidergram or flow chart to record the main events of this chapter and how they connect, both within the chapter and to other parts of the novel. For example, Meena lost the necklace in Chapter 5, and now it has re-entered the plot. We have also seen Sam's racism earlier – remind yourself where. The coming of the M6 now enables him to publicise his views on local TV. It also brings the unfortunate Indian man to Tollington. Meena's crisis comes as a result of overhearing Anita boasting about the attack.

CHECKPOINT 7 (A01)

Describe what has happened to the diamond necklace so far.

KEY LANGUAGE: SYAL'S USE OF IMAGERY (A02)

Syal makes much use of **imagery**. For example, in the first paragraph she emphasises Meena's unawareness in an **extended metaphor**: 'I ... let the days drift by unmarked, content to bob aimlessly along in the current, not bothering to appreciate the landscape' (p. 259). This expression of childhood innocence fits with the summer seeming 'blissfully carefree' (p. 265), and with the skylarks' **metaphorical** 'scimitar swoops of joy' (p. 266) – although perhaps this sword image hints at trouble to come, as does Mama's 'snake's nest of necklaces' (p. 267). The coming end of Meena's innocence is expressed metaphorically in the appearance of 'the cracks ... which would finally split open the china blue bowl of that last summer' (pp. 274–5).

CHAPTER 12: MEENA IN HOSPITAL

SUMMARY

- It is August, and Meena is in hospital recovering from her broken leg. Mama and Papa visit. Meena tries to 'erase' her memory of Anita (p. 282). She feels that she fell from Trixie deliberately, and resolves to be a better person.

- Meena gets to know Robert, a boy in an isolation room next to her. He is not allowed visitors, so they hold notes up to the glass. After a while they write in code.

- Robert is becoming Meena's boyfriend, but it is not the romance she once imagined.

- The family cannot now visit India, so Nanima is returning alone.

- Robert has painful medical tests and is declining. When Nurse Sylvie arranges for Meena to meet him properly, they are both surprised by each other's accents. Meena is awkward but feels connected to him.

- Meena comes home at Christmas to find the M6 built and new houses planned. She sees Anita kiss Sam on his new motorbike. She writes to Robert, then hears he has died.

KEY CONTEXT (A03)

Meena has 'tried to read and found too dense' *To Kill a Mockingbird* (p. 296). Like *Anita and Me*, it has a female narrator looking back on herself as a rebellious girl, explores the themes of racism and growing up, and features an eerie house with a mystery resident.

WHY IS THIS CHAPTER IMPORTANT?

A It shows Meena **surviving** without Anita, forming her **first relationship with a boy**, and recovering in **hospital** after four months.

B It shows Meena **changing** – resolving to become a **better person**, and **freeing herself** from **Anita**. It also shows change happening in other ways.

C It reveals that Meena **fell** from Trixie **deliberately** – or at least that she thinks she did.

D It presents Meena **enduring major losses** – Anita's friendship, Nanima and Robert.

KEY SETTING: THE HOSPITAL (A02)

This is the only chapter set almost entirely away from Tollington, signifying a break from Meena's normal influences – especially Anita. This encourages her to grow up in various ways. She is mildly scornful of the Good Hope Children's Ward, with its 'peeling yellow walls' (p. 280) and childish cartoon characters with speech bubbles, of her 'dopey looking' neighbour, and of a nurse who calls her Mary. Its one positive feature is Robert.

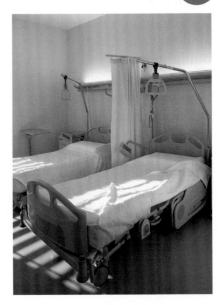

TOP TIP: WRITING ABOUT MEENA'S SEPARATION FROM ANITA A01

Read the description of Meena's separation from Anita on page 282. You will detect several stages in this change. First Meena reflects on how unconcerned Anita is about the riding accident: 'Anita had merely looked bored ... she closed her face like the end of a chapter in a long epic book.' She is beginning to realise that Anita never cared about her. At first she blames Anita for her broken leg 'totally', but gradually the hospital routine, together with her physical discomfort, makes her forget Anita. Write about what her language implies. When Meena says, 'I began to realise I could use this enforced separation wisely' to 'erase' Anita, her use of 'wisely' shows that she finally realises Anita is bad for her.

KEY QUOTATION: MEENA'S ACCIDENT A02

Commenting on the fall from Trixie that broke her leg, Meena says: 'I knew it had been a deliberate act, as deliberate as any of the lies I had told. Uncle Alan had been right all along; sin always had consequences' (p. 284). This is significant, but open to interpretation. At times lying has come so naturally to her that she can barely help it, so does that mean she made herself fall from the horse, but somehow could not help doing so? And does she see the fall as a sin, or as the consequence of her sins? If you write about this, you need to decide on your interpretation and support it with reference to the text.

> **CHECKPOINT 8** A01
>
> What learning experiences does Meena have in hospital?

KEY CHARACTER: ROBERT A02

Robert is not a major character, but Syal presents him with enough depth to make him realistic as someone to whom Meena would be drawn, and who can make her time in hospital bearable. He makes the first move towards Meena, thoughtfully writing 'Hi!!!' (p. 280) on the glass backwards so she will be able to read it. His being 'painfully thin' (p. 283) shows his illness, but his 'energetic, electric blue eyes' suggest force of character. He has a sense of humour, laughing about Angela, and playfully imitating Meena's accent. But he can also  be serious, as in the emotional moment when he holds her hand and implies that she is his 'girlfriend' (p. 292). We hear from Nurse Sylvie that his illness depresses him, but most of the time he seems courageously cheerful.

CHAPTER 13: DRAMATIC CLIMAX AT HOLLOW PONDS

SUMMARY

- Meena comments on change: the Bartlett estate is spreading; children must commute to school; motorway lights compete with the stars; teenagers occupy the park in the evenings; Tracey has become ghostlike.

- Meena's plaster cast is removed. Papa worries that she is unhappy, but she actually feels contented.

- Sam and Anita's taunting messages distract Meena from revising. She feels under pressure to pass her eleven-plus exam. The night before the exam, Tracey arrives, desperate, and leads Meena to Hollow Ponds – where Anita is having sex with Sam.

- Anita sees Sam kiss Meena, and throws rocks at them. When he raises his fist to Anita, Tracey launches herself at him but falls in the pond.

- Meena runs to the Big House for help and finds that its owners are not British: Mr Singh is Indian and his wife, Mireille, is French. Tracey 'dies' but is resuscitated. The police question Meena, who tells them the truth.

- Hari at the Big House advises Papa to sell the family home, and returns Mama's lost necklace. The Kumars move away. Meena leaves Anita a note saying she is going to the grammar school.

CHECKPOINT 9 **A01**

What losses have contributed to Meena growing up over the course of the novel?

KEY CONTEXT **A03**

Sam Lowbridge is committing a criminal act by having sex with Anita, because she is under 16 – probably 13, or 14 at most. He is at least 17: he must be this old to ride a motorbike.

WHY IS THIS CHAPTER IMPORTANT?

A It brings the novel to a **dramatic** climax which **tests** Meena and shows her **new maturity**.

B It **uncovers** the **mystery** of the **Big House** and its inhabitants.

C It **concludes** Meena's **relationship** with Anita, and **resolves** her double-edged **relationship** with Sam.

D It uses several **literary techniques**, such as withholding information.

E It **ends** the novel with Meena moving on to the **next stage** of her life.

KEY FORM: WITHHOLDING INFORMATION   **A02**

Syal withholds information on pages 310–11 to keep us guessing and to make us feel that the information, when it is finally revealed, will be highly significant, even shocking. Meena says that, on arriving at the pond with Tracey, she 'could see them in the clearing': she does not identify 'them'. In the next paragraph she says, 'He was on top of her, moving slightly.' This still conceals their identity, and only hints that they are having sex, which reproduces Meena's viewpoint: she would probably not know immediately what was happening, especially by moonlight. The next sentence identifies Anita, but Sam's identity is revealed only gradually, by his 'stubbly scalp, and ... a scar'.

TOP TIP: WRITING ABOUT STREAM OF CONSCIOUSNESS (A01)

This chapter employs a technique sometimes used as a novel approaches its climax: stream of consciousness. First Meena keeps repeating 'I Have An Exam Tomorrow. Tomorrow I Have An Exam' to focus her mind, as if repeating a 'mantra' – a phrase used in meditation (pp. 309–10). She begins to use this again on page 312, and then in a sentence that attempts to reproduce a lifelike 'stream' of thoughts coming in quick succession: 'Where was the path, who was nearest, phone the police somebody, which was the way out, every moment on dry land is another one underwater, I Have An Exam Tomorrow ...' (p. 315). This jumble of only loosely connected thoughts conveys Meena's anxiety and sense of urgency. The technique creates tension and suspense.

KEY CHARACTERS: MEENA AND SAM (A02)

Meena has always had a confused relationship with Sam. Early on she comments that, despite being 'the Yard's Bad Boy' (p. 55), he has always been 'polite, even kind to her' (p. 56), but she shuns him when it becomes clear that he is a racist, especially after his attack on the Indian man. Here she admits that she has 'secretly cast him all these years' as 'Sam Lowbridge the Hero ... the misunderstood rebel with a soul' (p. 311). She now sees him as 'Sam the Idiot', a blustering 'puppet' (p. 313). It is surprising when he tells her, 'Yow've always been the best wench in Tollington', and even more so when he kisses her for 'five seconds' (p. 314) without her objecting – not least as he must be over 17 and she is only 11. This kiss makes her feel victorious over him.

TOP TIP (A02)

Notice how Syal uses the device of overhearing to reveal information. In Chapter 12 this is how Meena discovers that Sam attacked the Indian man while Anita watched. In Chapter 13 she overhears her parents discussing her state of mind, and her eleven-plus exam (pp. 302–3).

KEY CONTEXT (A03)

In both *Anita and Me* and Harper Lee's *To Kill a Mockingbird* the feared inhabitants of a mystery house observe local children from afar and eventually turn out to be kind-hearted lifesavers. Mrs Singh, 'the witch' (p. 315), calls the ambulance that saves Tracey's life.

PROGRESS AND REVISION CHECK

SECTION ONE: CHECK YOUR KNOWLEDGE

Answer these quick questions to test your basic knowledge of the novel, its characters and events:

1. Why does Papa take Meena to Mr Ormerod's shop?

2. What is the 'Rickshaw Story' (p. 36) about?

3. Who is furious when Anita and Meena 'whoop' loudly down a passageway, and why?

4. What has Sam Lowbridge acquired 'by the age of sixteen' (p. 55)?

5. When and where did Papa unwittingly deliver a bomb?

6. What festival coincides with the fair coming to Tollington, and when?

7. What does Mama have to give the Mad Mitchells?

8. What is Anita and Meena's gang called?

9. Who opens the Tollington village fete?

10. How does Reverend Ince think the fete takings should be spent?

11. Who arrives home in an unfamiliar car while the Kumars are having a party?

12. What language does 'Mr Topsy' unexpectedly speak?

13. Where does Anita have a fight with Fat Sally?

14. Why does Meena try, unsuccessfully, to comfort Anita?

15. How does Sam Lowbridge publicise his racist views?

16. What is the name of Sherrie's horse?

17. What does Meena try to 'erase' (p. 282) in hospital?

18. Name the nurse who helps Meena to meet Robert properly.

19. What is odd about Meena when she has her plaster cast removed?

20. Why does Tracey throw herself into the pond?

PROGRESS AND REVISION CHECK

SECTION TWO: CHECK YOUR UNDERSTANDING

Here are two tasks that require more thought and slightly longer responses. In each case, try to write at least three to four paragraphs.

Task 1: What does Pinky and Baby's visit to the Kumars reveal or confirm about Meena? Think about:

- Meena's attitude towards Pink and Baby
- how she treats them

Task 2: Reread from 'It all started because of Anita's new bra' (p. 275) to the end of Chapter 11. How does Meera Syal reveal important information about Anita in this section, and how does it affect Meena? Think about:

- what facts are revealed about Anita, and how
- what this information makes Meena feel and do

PROGRESS CHECK

GOOD PROGRESS

I can:

- understand how Syal has sequenced and revealed events. ☐
- refer to the importance of key events in the novel. ☐
- select well-chosen evidence, including key quotations, to support my ideas. ☐

EXCELLENT PROGRESS

I can:

- refer in depth to main and minor events and how they contribute to the development of the plot. ☐
- understand how Syal has carefully ordered or revealed events for particular effects. ☐
- draw on a range of carefully selected key evidence, including quotations, to support my ideas. ☐

WHO'S WHO?

Nanima

Shyam Kumar
(Papa)

Daljit Kumar
(Mama)

Roberto Rutter

Deirdre Rutter

Sunil

Meena

Anita

Tracey

Aunties & Uncles

Sam Lowbridge

Sherrie & Fat Sally

Robert

Mrs Worrall

Mr Christmas

Uncle Alan, the
youth leader

Mr Ormerod, the
shopkeeper

MEENA

MEENA'S ROLE IN THE NOVEL

As the **first-person narrator**, Meena is the character who tells the story, and through whom our impressions of all the other characters are filtered. She is Daljit and Shyam's daughter, Sunil's sister, and Anita's friend. During the novel she:

- tells us about her parents, their friends and relatives, and their backgrounds.
- describes Tollington and its inhabitants.
- presents herself as an imaginative girl who lies to get what she wants, to get out of trouble, and to make life interesting.
- reveals what it is like to feel caught between the cultures of her middle-class Indian parents and her working-class English friend.
- shares with us her craving for drama, and her fantasies about romance and fame.
- becomes friends with Anita, whom she admires, then pities, then rejects.
- describes what she does with Anita, such as going to the fair, trespassing in the Big House grounds, stealing, going to the fete, and finally breaking her leg.
- sees Anita having sex with Sam, kisses Sam herself, and helps to save Tracey's life.

MEENA'S IMPORTANCE TO THE NOVEL AS A WHOLE

The novel describes two years in Meena's life which were important in her growing up, a major part of which was her relationship with Anita. Though only nine at the start of the novel, Meena narrates the story, with

numerous **digressions** from the main plot, from the perspective of her adult self, though we learn almost nothing about the adult she becomes. Apart from the Preface, the only explicit acknowledgement of this later adult self is when Meena comments, 'I have still never been able to say sorry without wanting to swallow the words as they sit on my tongue' (p. 60).

Meena often describes her childhood self with adult **irony** and understanding. She presents a picture of a troubled 'tomboy' (p. 302) who loves her parents but is aware of disappointing them. For much of the novel she feels a sense of not really belonging anywhere. This is perhaps why she has such a need for Anita's attention and approval.

TOP TIP (A02)

Remember that Meena reveals her character by how she chooses to tell the story. Syal also withholds some information, both to create suspense, and in keeping with Meena's limited awareness at the time – for example, about the mystery figure behind the Big House fence.

EXAM FOCUS: WRITING ABOUT MEENA

Key point	Evidence/Further meaning
● Meena is imaginative.	● She imagines trees around the Big House talking to her 'urgently' (p. 13). ● While Papa is trying to warn her about lying, she fantasises about being on *Opportunity Knocks* 'in lime hot pants and blonde hair', singing so brilliantly that the presenter sobs (p. 70).
● She is perceptive, sensitive, and sometimes compassionate.	● She knows that her father hates 'public shame ... more than anything' (p. 22). ● She tries to comfort Anita when Deirdre walks out (p. 247). ● She realises Anita needs her 'maybe more than I needed her' (p. 242).
● She is shocked, hurt and angered by racism.	● 'I backed off as if I had been punched' (p. 97). ● 'I felt as if I had been punched in the stomach' (p. 193).
● She can be very dishonest, but in the end chooses honesty.	● She lies about stealing money for sweets, and accuses Baby of stealing the collection tin (p. 159). ● She considers lying to the police about Tracey's near-death, but then explains, 'Tracey went for Sam and missed him and fell into the water' (p. 326).

CHECKPOINT 10 (A01)

On what occasions does Meena lie?

KEY QUOTATION: MEENA'S NEED FOR DRAMA (A02)

Immediately after Meena has overheard her parents discussing her, she comments: 'Ah, my darling parents, how much they had tried to cushion me from anything unpleasant or unusual, never guessing that this would only make me seek out the thrill of the dark and dramatic' (p. 303). Calling them 'darling' suggests a faintly **ironic** pity for their well-meaning but doomed attempts to protect her. At this point Meena is looking back with self-understanding at ways in which she looked for trouble. She has been naively envious of her parents' dramatic pasts in India,

asking herself, 'When would anything dangerous and cruel ever happen to me?' (p. 37). By pursuing a friendship with Anita she has unwittingly courted danger, and she sees herself as having deliberately broken her own leg by riding Trixie. In the end she sees life's 'cruel' losses, such as Robert and Nanima, as contributing to her growing up and learning self-acceptance: they are character-building.

ANITA

ANITA'S ROLE IN THE NOVEL

Anita is Deirdre and Roberto Rutter's daughter, Tracey's sister, and Meena's best friend for two years. At the start of the novel she is already at the local comprehensive school. During the novel she:

- begins the friendship with Meena, after testing her toughness.
- encourages Meena to behave more adventurously – or badly, for example when they upset Mr Christmas by 'whooping', or when they both steal from the shop.
- dominates and manipulates other children, including Meena, and bullies Tracey.
- demonstrates a love of adventure, enjoying the fair rides and leading Meena into the Big House grounds.
- flirts with youths who work at the fair, and tells Meena about sex.
- becomes Sam's girlfriend and enjoys watching him carry out a racist attack.
- shows vulnerability when her mother walks out.

ANITA'S IMPORTANCE TO THE NOVEL AS A WHOLE

As suggested by the novel's title, Anita is a major character because of her influence on Meena. She is older than Meena, already at secondary school. Meena calls her 'the undisputed "cock" of our yard' (p. 38), implying that no other child dares challenge her dominance. However, the fact that she befriends a younger girl points to her being in some ways immature, and needing someone she can dominate. In part, she represents white working-class Midlands culture, and her example encourages Meena to identify with this culture rather than that of her parents.

Anita is a complex character. She comes from a deprived background, with neglectful parents – a father who is probably abusive, and a promiscuous mother who abandons the family. She also represents a type of racism, admiring Sam's views but lacking the intelligence to see how they might affect Meena. She is perhaps at her best on horseback – riding without reins in a way that symbolises her own unrestrained character, naturally in tune with the animal and totally fearless.

EXAM FOCUS: WRITING ABOUT ANITA

Key point	Evidence/Further meaning
● Anita gets what she wants, whether by simple dominance or manipulation.	● She begins her friendship with Meena by snatching her sweets and walking off, 'shouting over her shoulder, "Yow coming then?"' (p. 38). ● She goads Fat Sally into attacking her, and then defeats her by calmly digging her nails into Fat Sally's face.
● She is self-confident and daring.	● She has no fear of adults, boldly stealing from Mr Ormerod, challenging Mr Christmas, and trespassing in the Big House grounds. ● Anita 'rode better than anyone else because she truly had no fear' (p. 242).
● She is in some ways naive.	● She thinks the fairground youth ('the Poet') cares for her, and is unaware of him having sex with her mother (p. 123). ● She believes that her parents will buy her a pony (p. 99).
● She can be self-centred, thoughtless and cruel.	● She bullies Tracey, as when she taunts her for having a 'poo stripe' (p. 141), and threatens her: 'I swear I'll kill yow' (p. 276). ● She is insensitive to Meena's likely feelings about racism, and enjoys watching Sam beat up an Indian man.

TOP TIP: ANITA'S EFFECT ON OTHERS (A01)

Notice the powerful effect that Anita has on others. From the start, Meena feels 'privileged to be in her company' (p. 38). She says, 'I never had to force my admiration, it flowed from every pore because Anita made me laugh like no one else' (p. 138). However, Anita also rules others with 'pre-pubescent feminine wiles, pouting, sulking, clumsy cack-handed flirting and unsettling mood swings' (p. 39). Her flirting turns the fairground 'boy-men ... into grinning, pliant pets' (p. 104). Even Sam is 'under Anita's spell' (p. 313).

AIMING HIGH: A FULLY ROUNDED CHARACTER ⭐

For higher marks, show that you can see the contradictions in Anita's character – her positive traits as well as the negative. For example, when she first engages Meena in conversation (p. 38), she seems to have a genuinely childlike curiosity about the butterfly eggs, but then strips the leaves off the twig and flicks it at Meena. She also has a real enthusiasm for Meena's clothes, and tries to smuggle some of them out of the Kumars' house.

CHECKPOINT 11 (A01)

What evidence is there of Anita's vulnerability?

DALJIT KUMAR (MAMA)

MAMA'S ROLE IN THE NOVEL

Mama is Nanima's daughter, Shyam's wife and the mother of Meena, and later Sunil. She is also a primary-school teacher. She was born in an Indian village, then moved to Delhi. During the novel she:

- provides a role model for Meena, in her grace, courtesy to neighbours, kindness and opposition to prejudice.
- is often unhappy, missing India and finding English attitudes towards immigrants difficult.
- is a generous hostess to the Aunties and Uncles.
- is exasperated by Meena's lies.
- drives Meena to the Sikh temple.
- gives birth to Sunil by emergency caesarean section.
- becomes exhausted and close to a breakdown, but is relieved when Nanima visits.
- is kind but firm with Anita when her mother leaves.

KEY CONTEXT **A03**

Meena compares Mama 'in a strop' (p. 27) to the fierce Hindu goddess Kali, best-known as the goddess of destruction, and often pictured wearing a necklace of human heads or skulls.

EXAM FOCUS: WRITING ABOUT MAMA

A01

Key point	Evidence/Further meaning
• Mama is sometimes moodily unhappy.	• Her 'moods had begun to intrude upon every family outing like a fourth silent guest' (p. 25). • After Sunil's birth: 'Her tearful door slammings and tantrums had gradually disappeared, to be replaced with long, exhausted silences or more frightening blank stares' (p. 171).
• She is warm, unless offended, considerate and polite to a fault.	• She is offended by Deirdre's name for her poodle: 'From that day on, mama decided that Deirdre would not be one of the many beneficiaries of her impeccable manners and warm social chit-chat' (p. 90). • She offers the Mitchells a lift, not expecting them to accept, then washes out Cara's 'small patch of urine' (p. 114) at night to avoid embarrassing them.
• She is devoted to Meena and does her best for her.	• She drives Meena to the Sikh temple to learn about the religion, despite her lack of confidence as a driver. • Upset by Meena's broken leg, she remains supportive: 'She was calm now, in control, she would not let me down' (p. 281).
• She can be upset by Meena.	• She cannot understand Meena's lying: '"Why do you do this, Meena?" she would wail, wringing her hands' (p. 28). • When Meena suggests putting Sunil in an orphanage, 'Her reply was to burst into tears and rush into her bedroom' (p. 169).

SHYAM KUMAR (PAPA)

PAPA'S ROLE IN THE NOVEL

Papa is Daljit's husband, and the father of Meena and Sunil. He works in an office, probably as an accountant. He comes from Lahore, in what is now Pakistan. During the novel he:

- takes Meena to the village shop to find out whether she stole money to buy sweets.
- tries to warn Meena about the consequences of lying.
- enjoys singing at musical evenings and encourages Meena to do so.
- tries to soothe his wife.
- talks about his experiences in India during Partition.
- copes with flirtatious local women attracted by his good looks.
- worries about Meena and is hurt that she talks to him less as she gets older.
- sometimes gets angry with Meena, as when she asks if she is a virgin.
- does a job he does not enjoy, eventually getting promoted.

CHECKPOINT 12 A01

In what ways do you think Papa is a good father?

EXAM FOCUS: WRITING ABOUT PAPA

Key point	Evidence/Further meaning
• Papa is a patient, caring father.	• He gives Meena a chance to prove that she did not steal, and is disappointed to find she was lying (p. 23). • He tries to explain to Meena why lying is bad by telling her the story of 'the boy and the tiger' (p. 70).
• He is a loving husband.	• He tries to comfort Daljit when she is unhappy: 'Papa found her on the bed, crying. He'd said it was a migraine and then talked softly to her in Punjabi' (p. 24). • He wonders what Daljit saw in him. Like her, he thinks he is 'the lucky one' (p. 82).
• He is a sensitive and inspiring musician.	• He sings, 'notes ... so close in tone but each one different, a gradual ascent and then pure flight' (p. 72). • Meena asks, 'what word would there be for these feelings that papa's songs awoke in everyone?' (p. 72)
• He is enterprising, determined and hard-working.	• From being 'in a refugee camp with only what I stood up in' (p. 75), he has earned qualifications, come to England and secured a professional job. • Every day he returns from work 'with a bulging briefcase full of papers covered with minute indecipherable figures' (p. 83).

NANIMA

NANIMA'S ROLE IN THE NOVEL

Nanima is Mama's mother. She lives in India and returns there towards the end of the novel. During the novel she visits the family and:

- helps Mama with Sunil and makes him less dependent on Mama.
- communicates well with Meena, despite speaking little English.
- is like a loving second mother to Meena.
- shares a bed with Meena.
- seems to appreciate Meena's wild character.
- tells dramatic stories about her life in India.

EXAM FOCUS: WRITING ABOUT NANIMA

Key point	Evidence/Further meaning
● Nanima is a confident, independent woman.	● She takes the initiative to visit and befriend the Worralls. ● She goes into Mr Ormerod's shop and does the shopping, despite speaking little or no English.
● She has a connection with Meena and appreciates her.	● She pats Meena under the chin 'conspiratorially' (p. 200). ● Nanima 'dragged me under her arm … Then she opened one eye briefly and said, "Junglee!" before dropping off to sleep' (p. 207).
● She is a talented teller of colourful stories about India that give Meena a sense of belonging.	● 'Most of all I enjoyed her stories' (p. 209). ● She makes Meena see India as 'a country … bursting with excitement, drama and passion, history in the making' (p. 211).
● A good judge of character, she perceives that Anita is bad for Meena.	● Meena notes, 'whilst my parents did their dance of welcome around Anita … my Nanima remained singularly uninvolved and unimpressed' (p. 254). ● Meena realises that 'Nanima had not taken to my best friend' (p. 255).

TOP TIP: WRITING ABOUT NANIMA A01

Since Nanima speaks little English, and Meena's understanding of Punjabi is limited, our impression of Nanima is formed largely by her actions. For example, her unpredictable tidying of household items into unfamiliar places shows that she wants to help, but makes her own decisions about where things go. Her tying of a thread around Sunil's wrist shows her protectiveness and her superstition.

TOP TIP A01

If you write an exam essay on Nanima, you will need to focus on Chapters 8–11.

THE AUNTIES AND UNCLES

THE ROLE OF THE AUNTIES AND UNCLES IN THE NOVEL

The Aunties and Uncles are Indian friends of the Kumars, not blood relatives, but like an extended family. During the novel they:

- visit the Kumars for social and musical gatherings (*mehfils*).
- shower Meena with affection but also criticise her like parents.
- discuss their Indian personal histories, overheard by Meena.
- help to welcome Nanima.

Shaila is the only one who is developed as a character. She is the mother of Pinky and Baby, and the wife of Uncle Amman. During the novel she:

- prays at her shrine and explains the Hindu belief in reincarnation to Meena.
- attracts attention by being outspoken and entertaining.
- disciplines, praises and protects Meena.
- helps with food at gatherings and when Mama collapses.
- punishes Pinky and Baby unfairly.
- phones the Kumars, upset, when Amman has a heart attack.

CHECKPOINT 13 A01

How does Shaila stand out from the other Aunties as a character?

EXAM FOCUS: WRITING ABOUT SHAILA AND THE AUNTIES AND UNCLES

Key point	Evidence/Further meaning
• The Aunties and Uncles are a support to the Kumars.	• 'I knew how intensely my parents valued these people they so readily renamed as family' (p. 31). • They exchange 'anecdotes that reinforced their shared histories' (p. 31).
• Their tragic stories have a powerful effect on Meena.	• 'I felt a hundred other memories were being briefly relived and battened down again' (p. 74).
• Meena is fond of Shaila and sees her as a fun-loving, extrovert character.	• 'The fattest, noisiest and most fun ... she could only express herself in extremes of emotion, banshee howls of disbelief or ear-splitting yodels of joy' (p. 74).
• Shaila is a firm and sometimes impassioned disciplinarian.	• She makes Meena remove her make-up after she defies Papa: 'Now upstairs, and come back down wearing your own pretty face' (p. 109). • Wrongly thinking that Baby is a thief, she hits her 'soundly on the back of her head' then slaps 'any bit of Pinky that came within reach' (p. 161).

DEIRDRE AND TRACEY RUTTER

THE ROLES OF DEIRDRE AND TRACEY IN THE NOVEL

Deirdre is the mother of Anita and Tracey, and the unfaithful wife of Roberto. During the novel she:

- decides not to invite Meena for tea.
- gives her poodle an offensive name.
- appears to be having an affair, and probably has sex with Anita's 'boyfriend'.
- abandons the family.

Tracey is Anita's younger sister. During the novel she:

- hangs around with Anita when she is allowed to.
- is bullied by Anita.
- is probably being abused.
- reveals that Anita is seeing Sam Lowbridge.
- takes Meena to Hollow Ponds the night before Meena's eleven-plus exam.
- jealously tries to protect Anita and almost drowns in the pond.

CHECKPOINT 14 (A01)

What evidence is there that Deirdre is a bad mother?

EXAM FOCUS: WRITING ABOUT DEIRDRE AND TRACEY (A01)

Key point	Evidence/Further meaning
• Deirdre is a mysterious and rather threatening character.	• Her lips 'always on the edge of a sneer' and sharp teeth give her 'an expression of dark, knowing hunger' (p. 55). • She makes the tough Anita burst into tears with 'a few short barking phrases' (p. 206).
• Tracey is a victim.	• She is bullied by Anita, as when Anita encourages the other children to mock her (p. 141). • It is hinted that she is being abused: bruises on her thighs show 'the imprint of ten cruel, angry fingers' (p. 142).
• Despite being mistreated, Tracey is fiercely loyal and protective – or possessive.	• She throws herself at Sam when he raises his fist to Anita, 'leaping at Sam like a terrier' and 'flying through the air' with no thought for her own safety (p. 314).

SAM LOWBRIDGE

THE ROLE OF SAM LOWBRIDGE IN THE NOVEL

Sam is the son of single-parent Glenys, and has a criminal record. During the novel he:

- heckles Reverend Ince, criticising plans to spend the fete takings on the chapel roof, then becoming racist.
- is televised shouting a racist slogan into a news camera.
- is polite and kind to Meena, helping her win a bracelet.
- becomes a skinhead, rides a moped, then a motorbike.
- beats up and robs an Indian man.
- with Anita, leaves anonymous notes for Meena.
- has sex with Anita, then kisses Meena.

EXAM FOCUS: WRITING ABOUT SAM LOWBRIDGE

Key point	Evidence/Further meaning
• Sam has a reputation as a delinquent.	• He is 'the wild boy of the yard (he'd already been up for shoplifting and nicking bikes)' (p. 49).
• He likes Meena.	• Meena says: 'Most of the littl'uns were scared of him ... but ... he'd always been polite, even kind, to me' (pp. 55–6). • He helps Meena win a bracelet at the fair, and eventually tells her: 'Yow've always been the best wench in Tollington. Anywhere! Dead funny' (p. 314).
• He is a racist, despite liking Meena.	• He makes a scene at the fete when he protests about charity going to 'darkies' (p. 193), and later shouts, 'If You Want A ... For A Neighbour, Vote Labour!' into a news camera (p. 273). • His attack on the Indian man is likely to be racially motivated.
• He is in some ways a victim, or at least a loser in life.	• Meena sees him as being controlled by Anita: 'For all his bluster ... Sam was truly nothing more than a puppet' (p. 313). • He feels that he is not good enough for Meena, and that she will 'move on' while he is unable to: 'How come I can't?' (p. 314).

TOP TIP (A01)

As with Anita, try to see how Sam is presented as a fully rounded character, not just a negative one.

MINOR CHARACTERS

THE ROLE OF MINOR CHARACTERS IN THE NOVEL

Minor characters include Mr Ormerod the shopkeeper, Uncle Alan, and the Worralls and Christmases. They represent the Tollington community, an English counterpart to the Aunties and Uncles. In addition, Sherrie and Fat Sally interact with Anita, revealing her character.

- Mr Ormerod collects for charity. Anita and Meena steal from him and he visits the Kumars when he finds out.
- Uncle Alan supports the community. He runs a Sunday School and youth groups. He urges Sam to channel his anger more positively.
- Mrs Worrall looks after her disabled husband. She shows Meena how to make jam tarts. She tells Mama she should take Nanima out more.
- Mr Christmas shouts at Anita and Meena for 'whooping' in the passageway.
- Sherrie comes from a relatively wealthy family and lets Anita ride her pony, Trixie.
- Fat Sally is goaded by Anita into a fight which Anita wins.
- Mr Singh is Indian, his name revealing that he is a Sikh like Meena's mother. The fact that he could afford to buy the mine, and still lives in the Big House, makes him unusual for an immigrant at this time, as does his marriage to a non-Indian – a French woman.

KEY CONTEXT **A03**

In the 1960s and 1970s, many children went to a church-run Sunday school on Sunday morning, like the one Uncle Alan runs, even if their parents were not particularly religious.

EXAM FOCUS: WRITING ABOUT MINOR CHARACTERS **A01**

Key point	Evidence/Further meaning
• Mr Ormerod is well-meaning, but patronising towards other ethnic groups.	• Meena calls drivers reversing for her mother 'an act of benevolence ... as well-intentioned as any of Mr Ormerod's charity parcels to the poor children in Africa' (p. 97). • On overseas charity, he says: 'it's not just about giving them stuff, is it? It's about giving them culture as well, civilisation' (p. 172).
• Uncle Alan is normally positive and enthusiastic, but he can become angry.	• He comes 'bounding across the yard ... eager and slobbery as a Labrador' seeking volunteers for his 'good egg schemes' (p. 41). • He is furious with Reverend Ince: 'to see him so contorted with anger made him almost unrecognisable' (p. 179).
• Elderly Mr Christmas and Mrs Worrall are devoted to their spouses.	• Mr Christmas shouts at Anita and Meena for disturbing his sick wife – and keeps her body in the house after she dies. • Mrs Worrall has looked after her disabled husband on her own, uncomplainingly, for 'twenty-two years' (p. 66).
• Sherrie and Fat Sally are manipulated and dominated by Anita.	• 'Anita leading the way with Sherrie or Fat Sally at her side, favoured and blessed, whilst the scapegoat of the hour sulked and straggled behind' (p. 88). • Meena speaks of Sherrie and Fat Sally doing 'their merry dance of repulsion and attraction around Anita' (p. 187).

PROGRESS AND REVISION CHECK

SECTION ONE: CHECK YOUR KNOWLEDGE

TOP TIP (A01)

Answer these quick questions to test your basic knowledge of the novel's characters.

1 What kind of school does Uncle Alan run?

2 Who does Sandy marry?

3 What is the first thing that Anita ever tells Meena?

4 Why is Papa disappointed by Meena at the start of the novel?

5 What does Daljit do to shock Papa so that he asks what she is doing (p. 106)?

6 Who does Mr Topsy speak to in Punjabi?

7 What does Mrs Worrall show Meena?

8 Why does Anita throw a rock at Sam Lowbridge?

9 Who has 'an expression of dark, knowing hunger' (p. 55)?

10 Who tries to comfort Anita, and why?

SECTION TWO: CHECK YOUR UNDERSTANDING

TOP TIP (A01)

This task requires more thought and a slightly longer response. Try to write at least three to four paragraphs.

Task: In what ways does Anita influence Meena? Think about:

● ways in which Anita is a bad influence or gets Meena into trouble
● other ways in which she influences Meena or makes her grow up

PROGRESS CHECK

GOOD PROGRESS

I can:

● explain the significance of the main characters in how the action develops. ☐
● refer to how they are described by Syal and how this affects the way we see them. ☐

EXCELLENT PROGRESS

I can:

● analyse in detail how Syal has shaped and developed characters over the course of the novel. ☐
● infer key ideas, themes and issues from the ways characters and relationships are presented by Syal. ☐

THEMES

FRIENDSHIP

Anita and Me could be called a novel about friendship, and Meena sees Anita as her 'best friend' (pp. 255, 274, 277, 324), and cares about her. But is Anita really Meena's friend? Consider:

- Anita's first words to Meena are a lie – she tells Meena that the sailor in a cigarette advert is her father (p. 17). This could be to impress Meena or just to belittle her.
- The real start of the friendship (p. 38) is when Anita shows Meena some butterfly eggs on a twig, then flicks it at Meena's legs to test her reaction. She walks off with Meena's sweets, expecting her to follow. This sets the **tone** for their relationship: Anita dominates; Meena feels privileged to be with her.
- Meena admires Anita. For example, when Anita charms the fairground youths, Meena is 'open-mouthed in admiration' (p. 104). Later Meena describes their conversations: 'Anita talked and I listened with the appropriate appreciative noises' (p. 138).
- Gradually Meena starts to see Anita's vulnerability. She protects Anita from Deirdre's betrayal with 'the Poet': 'at this moment I could not leave Anita alone' (p. 122). She feels 'pity' for Anita when Deirdre makes her cry (p. 206), and after Deirdre walks out (p. 247)
- The friendship starts to fall apart because of racism. Anita lacks the awareness to understand why Meena might be upset by Sam's racist heckling (p. 193), but the final blow comes when Meena overhears Anita boasting about the attack on an Indian man (p. 277).
- Anita never visits Meena in hospital, but Meena still leaves her a farewell note when the Kumars move away.

THEME TRACKER (A01)

Friendship

- p. 38: Anita walks off with Meena's sweets, assuming she will follow.
- p. 206: Meena feels pity for Anita when she sees Deirdre make her cry.
- p. 277: Meena finally realises the friendship cannot continue when she hears Anita boasting about a racist attack.

TOP TIP (A02)

Bear in mind that Anita's influence is not all bad. For example, she makes Meena more daring – as in 'whooping' in the passageway (p. 44) and going to see the Big House's Hindu statue. You could see these as moments when Anita generously shares something with a friend, or as further tests – or both.

AIMING HIGH: COMMENT ON MEENA'S FRIENDSHIP WITH ROBERT

During the course of the novel, Meena starts to become interested in boys, partly inspired by Anita, Sherrie and Fat Sally. Her ideas about love and romance are strongly influenced by *Jackie* magazine. However, her first real relationship with a boy is with Robert. Because they meet in hospital, with Robert in an isolation room, the relationship develops as a friendship, with no pressure to conform to a romantic ideal. Their friendship, based on notes held up to the glass partition, is established by the time they meet properly and speak for the first time. When they do meet,

Meena feels awkward, but she is moved by him implying that she is his girlfriend. Does he really feel this, or is he being kind?

CHECKPOINT 15 A01

List the occasions when Meena is a good friend to Anita.

KEY QUOTATION: MEENA, ANITA AND SAM   A01

After the climax in which Sam kisses Anita and Tracey nearly dies, Meena reflects on all that has happened: 'I had lost my best friend to someone who could have been a friend and lost himself' (p. 324). This suggests that Meena has jealously guarded her friendship with Anita, and felt that Anita could not have a boyfriend and still be her best friend – as if she had a 'crush' on Anita. It also implies that Meena thinks Sam could have been her friend – perhaps if he had not 'lost himself' to racism, or to a defeatism that makes him resent someone from an ethnic minority who has a career, unlike him.

REVISION FOCUS: HOW GOOD A FRIEND IS MEENA?

TOP TIP   A02

When Meena says, 'My best friend was sharing me with someone else' (p. 277), she really means that she, Meena, was sharing Anita with someone else.

- Use the bullet points in this section to remind yourself of what Meena gives, or offers, Anita during the course of their friendship – for example at the fair (p. 122).
- Now consider how good a friend Meena is to Pinky and Baby (pp. 150–61).

- Finally, consider what Meena contributes to her friendship with Robert (Ch. 12), and how this differs from her other friendships.
- Create a mind map or spidergram showing Meena's strengths and weaknesses as a friend.

FAMILY

Family is a backdrop to the theme of friendship in the novel. To some extent Meena rejects her family by choosing the friendship of white working-class Anita, along with at least some of her values. However, her family supports her throughout – in a way that contrasts with Anita's family:

- Meena's parents are loving and caring, but are exasperated by Meena's lies. They also have their own problems, which can at times make Meena feel excluded, as in her account of her seventh birthday (p. 27).

- Nanima greatly benefits the Kumars' family life. Meena becomes close to her at a time when Mama is preoccupied with Sunil, and it is partly because of Nanima that Meena comes to love Sunil rather than seeing him as a nuisance.

- The Kumars' supportive family life is contrasted with that of the Rutters. Anita seems to get little emotional support from her mother, who is unfaithful and eventually abandons her children. Tracey is probably being abused by Roberto (p. 142), and eventually becomes deeply insecure, and jealously possessive towards Anita.

- The Worralls are also contrasted with the Kumars. Mama thinks it is shameful that their children never visit them, despite living nearby (p. 58).

- Family is also explored through the Aunties and Uncles. Though not blood relations, they are important to the Kumars for their friendship, shared history, and shared experience as immigrants.

THEME TRACKER (A01)

Family

- p. 87: Meena resists the extension of the family unit she is used to, seeing the prospect of a brother or sister as a threat.

- p. 200: Meena immediately takes to Nanima, who becomes an important new source of love and family support to her.

- p. 247: Anita has not had much love and support from her mother, but is still upset when she leaves.

EXAM FOCUS: WRITING ABOUT EFFECTS (A02)

Here is what one student has written about the way Syal presents the Aunties and Uncles:

> Meena hates the traditionally Indian way the Aunties and Uncles 'continually interfered in my upbringing' – 'interfered' implying that they should leave her upbringing to her parents. However, there is affectionate humour in the alliterated metaphor she uses for their criticisms: 'This was a moral marathon, and they took up the baton with pride.' They are proud of their shared role, but perhaps also of Meena, as if she is their daughter too.' Their criticisms, more affectionate than serious, make Meena feel 'safe and wanted'. These simple adjectives suggest the uncomplicated sense of security that Meena gets from them.

Analyses an implicit meaning

Shows awareness of the cultural context

Correct use of a double technical term

Suggests a valid interpretation

Now you try it:

Add a sentence explaining how Meena realises the importance of the Aunties and Uncles to her parents. Start: *The Aunties and Uncles help…*

THEME TRACKER (A01)

Change and growing up

● p. 37: Meena longs for exciting change in her life. Immediately after this, her friendship with Anita begins.

● p. 185: The fortune-teller is strangely accurate in predicting change in Meena's life.

● p. 293: Meena returns from hospital, changed by her experience, to find that Tollington has changed in her absence.

KEY CONTEXT (A03)

A UK 'baby boom' took place in the 1960s, increasing the population. Added to this, the coming of the M6 made it easier for people to commute the 25 kilometres to Birmingham from Essington, on which Tollington is based, so it became more built up. We see this change reflected in the novel with the building of the new estate.

CHANGE AND GROWING UP

Meena is nine at the start of the novel and 11 by the end, so she still has more growing up to do. However, she changes significantly in these two years, partly because of Anita. Meanwhile, Tollington is also changing. Anita develops too, but less obviously. Consider how:

● The novel begins with Meena being caught lying, and this is not the last time. Perhaps her worst lie is when she blames her theft of the charity collection tin on Baby (p. 159). However, it is a turning point when she tells the police the truth about Tracey (p. 326).

● Meena begins by simply admiring Anita, but she gradually develops compassion for her. It is after Anita has behaved so badly towards Fat Sally that Meena realises 'She needed me maybe more than I needed her' and feels 'pity' for her (p. 242).

● Meena develops a sense of responsibility, coupled with a sense of justice. She cares for Nanima and confronts Mr Ormerod when she thinks he has cheated her grandmother. She also learns to love and care for Sunil.

● Meena comes to realise the consequences of her actions. Her broken leg means that the family cannot accompany Nanima to India.

● Anita does not change for the better: she just becomes more expertly manipulative and graduates from flirting to having sex with Sam. Tracey becomes more insecure and possessive.

AIMING HIGH: COMMENT ON CHANGE IN TOLLINGTON

If you are writing about the theme of change, remember that Meena's character develops against the backdrop of social change in Tollington. The village has already changed before the start of the novel. The mine has shut, so it is hard for men to find jobs, though women can work at the ballbearings factory. During the course of the novel the countryside round the village disappears and the M6 is built. Racism also develops, leading to Sam's attack on Rajesh Bhatra. Papa's promotion, which enables the Kumars to move to a better area, shows that educated immigrants are gradually achieving more status professionally, despite growing racism in Britain as a whole.

CULTURE

The theme of culture connects to those of family and racism. It is also central to Meena as a character, because she feels so rootless, and divided between her family's Indian culture and the white working-class culture around her:

- Culture includes values. *Anita and Me* shows contrasting family values. Indians value their relatives and support them. The Kumars form a substitute 'family' in the Aunties and Uncles. Family ties are weak in the local community, as shown by the elderly Worralls' children never visiting or helping with disabled Mr Worrall.

- The Aunties' and Uncles' comments on English habits also show cultural differences: 'all this garden frippery, gnomes, wells and the like, was an English thing' (p. 33).

- Culture also includes artistic expression. The Kumars' musical evenings keep alive the folk songs and *ghazals* (p. 71) from their Indian past. This is contrasted with English pop music when Meena sings 'We Wear Short Shorts', which is shallow by comparison.

- A third aspect of culture is food. Syal implies that Indian cuisine is superior to local English, though the latter is less time-consuming, and Meena prefers it. There is also a contrast in eating styles: Anita is shocked when the Kumars eat with their fingers.

- Meena is surprised and Papa excited to find that Mr Singh is Indian. His keeping himself to himself is unlike the sociable behaviour of Meena's parents and their friends.

TOP TIP: WRITING ABOUT COMIC DIFFERENCES (A02)

Note how cultural differences are sometimes a source of comedy in the novel. When Anita is presented with Indian food her graceless response shows her resistance to anything unfamiliar. She reacts 'as if confronted with a festering sheep's head on a platter' (p. 253). When Mr Ormerod is persuaded to try an Indian snack, he bites on a hot chilli and is described, with comic exaggeration, drinking from the tap, 'gulping like he'd just come back from a long desert trek' (p. 159). This is also amusingly **ironic**, given Mr Ormerod's patronising attitude to non-English cultures.

KEY QUOTATION: CLOTHES IN CULTURE (A01)

For Mama, 'looking glamorous in saris and formal Indian suits was part of the English people's education' (p. 25). She tends to see the English as culturally narrow-minded and in need of a broader outlook.

THEME TRACKER (A01)

Culture

- p. 92: The Kumars celebrate Diwali, but also make an effort to celebrate Christmas for Meena's sake.

- p. 211: Meena becomes interested in Indian culture through Nanima, and wants to visit India.

- p. 254: Mama and Papa conspire with Meena to persuade Anita that people eat with their fingers 'in all the top restaurants'.

KEY CONTEXT (A03)

'Short Shorts' was a very simple and repetitive 1958 pop song by US band the Royal Teens. It was covered by the British band Freddie and the Dreamers in 1966.

THEME TRACKER (A01)

Racism

- p. 97: The woman driver's racism makes Meena feel as if she has been 'punched', but she decides not to burden her parents with her feelings.

- p. 273: Sam publicises his racism by yelling a slogan into a TV camera.

- p. 277: Anita boasts to Sherrie about Sam's racist attack, perhaps by now realising that she should not tell Meena about it.

RACISM AND PREJUDICE

Meena gradually becomes aware of racism, and is then outraged by it. Syal presents it in a variety of forms:

- Meena's first encounter with racism is when she asks an elderly driver to reverse. The woman responds with abuse but speaks 'casually' (p. 97), implying that she barely thinks about the impact of her words.

- Sam Lowbridge is also thoughtlessly racist, unaware that his comments (p. 193) might affect Meena. Anita is similarly unaware. Sam progresses to racist violence when he attacks Rajesh Bhatra.

- Mr Ormerod is less obviously racist. He is a Christian and collects money for the African poor, but he also thinks that people in developing countries need 'a good, true way of living, like what we have' (p. 172).

- Mama says that local people accept the Kumars only because 'they don't think we are really Indian'. She resents being told she is 'so English' as if it is a 'compliment' (p. 172).

- The violence of Indian Partition, described by the Aunties and Uncles, is a kind of racism, since Hindus and Muslims tend to be from different ethnic groups rather than just having different religious beliefs.

- The Aunties and Uncles are mildly racist about the English: 'They don't like bathing, and when they do, they sit in their own dirty water instead of showering' (p. 33).

- At the time when the novel is set, the Troubles had begun in Northern Ireland, with violence between the Protestant and Catholic communities, and acts of terrorism on both sides. This could be compared with Hindu–Muslim violence in India.

KEY QUOTATION: MEENA'S OUTRAGE (A02)

Meena is most outraged about racism when she hears of it being directed at other people, like her tiny, gentle Auntie Usha. Thinking of her being pushed around by skinheads she feels 'both impotent and on fire' (p. 173). This description conveys a great tension between her righteous anger and her powerlessness to act on it.

TOP TIP (A02)

Be aware that Syal describes different types of racism and prejudice, from Mr Ormerod's patronising ignorance to Sam's resentful viciousness, and that some examples are open to interpretation. In particular, does Deirdre Rutter name her dog unaware of the name's racist overtones, as Papa thinks, or is Mama right to be offended?

CHECKPOINT 16 (A01)

What incidents make racism become more prominent in Tollington?

TRUTH AND FICTION

Anita and Me contains both lies and fantasies, mostly, but not all, coming from Meena:

- The novel opens with Meena's lie about being given sweets. She knows stealing is wrong, and feels ashamed, but still blames her father: 'if he had … just given me the … money, I would not have had to steal anything' (p. 21).

- Meena is a fantasist, for example imagining herself on *Opportunity Knocks*, while her father tells her a story to teach her not to lie (p. 70).

- Anita's first words to Meena are a lie – when she claims that the sailor in an advert is her father (p. 17). This identifies a similarity between the two girls.

- Meena experiences the truth of Papa's moral tale about 'the boy and the tiger' (p. 70) when she says that she saw Mrs Christmas on the day she was found dead. This is true (though she was already dead), but Mama assumes that Meena is lying again (p. 78).

- Hearing Nanima's stories helps to convince Meena that reality can be exciting, but she still tells the Ballbearings Women a ridiculous fabrication about Nanima speaking Russian, mining precious minerals, and fleeing from molten lava (p. 220).

- It is a significant moment when Meena realises that Anita is just fantasising about being bought a pony (p. 242).

- Meena ultimately chooses truth when she tells the police how Tracey nearly died, even though she could incriminate both Anita and Sam.

AIMING HIGH: AN UNRELIABLE NARRATOR? ⭐

The fact that Meena is based on Meera Syal herself, who lived as a child in Essington, on which Tollington is based, might make us wonder if Meena is meant to be an unreliable narrator. Syal does seem to play with the idea of fiction. For example, the Preface begins with 'the alternative history I trot out in job interview situations' (p. 9). Remember that this is the adult Meena speaking, not Syal herself. Syal also plays with the idea of fiction when Meena tells us what she plans to tell the police, before actually telling the truth (p. 324).

THEME TRACKER (A01)

Truth and fiction

- p. 28: Meena admits to lying about the stolen money. At this point she probably feels more guilty about the theft than the lie.

- p. 78: With Mrs Christmas's death, Meena begins to learn that habitual liars lose credibility.

- p. 326: Meena rejects revenge in favour of truth, leaving Sam and Anita 'to themselves'.

KEY CONTEXT (A03)

Like Scout, the narrator of *To Kill a Mockingbird*, Meena may be seen as an unreliable narrator for two reasons: a child would not understand all of the events, and an adult looking back might not remember them accurately.

CONTEXTS

MEERA SYAL AND ESSINGTON

Meera Syal calls *Anita and Me* 'semi-autobiographical'. However, it is safest for you to treat it as a work of fiction. Meena is based on Meera (only one letter different!), but they are not identical. Nonetheless, you should be aware of some similarities:

- Syal was born in the largely white working-class West Midlands village of Essington, near Wolverhampton, on which Tollington is based. Essington did have a coal mine, which was shut by the time Syal lived there. It still has ponds left over from mining activity.

- Syal's parents were Punjabi Indians who arrived from New Delhi, two years before Meera was born in 1961. Her father was Hindu, and an accountant (like Shyam); her mother was Sikh and a school teacher (like Daljit).

- According to Syal's mother, she liked to perform as a child. Meena performs 'Short Shorts' and dramatises herself in fantasies – imagining being on *Opportunity Knocks*. Meera Syal became a performer. She is probably more famous as an actress and comedian (*Goodness Gracious Me*, *The Kumars at No. 42*) than as a novelist.

- Syal says that there was no single 'Anita' in her childhood. She told the BBC: 'She was an amalgamation of two or three older girls in my village who I used to follow around.'

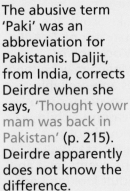

IMMIGRATION FROM INDIA AND PAKISTAN

The experiences of being an immigrant, and of being a second-generation immigrant (born in this country to immigrants), is central to *Anita and Me*. Here are the key facts:

- Immigration from India and what became Pakistan was historically based on most of India being ruled by Britain as a colony from 1848 to 1947. English became the official language of a country where many languages were spoken, including Punjabi.

- The UK government encouraged immigration from its colonies and former colonies (the Commonwealth) to help rebuild Britain after the Second World War.

- India became independent in 1947, its northern part becoming the Muslim state of Pakistan. During this Partition there was widespread violence as people fled in each direction, depending on their religion, especially in the Punjab. This was an added reason for emigration. Britain began to impose immigration controls only in 1962.

ENOCH POWELL AND RACISM

Be aware of the novel's political background. Enoch Powell (1912–88) was Conservative Shadow Secretary of State from 1965 to 1968. He was sacked by party leader Edward Heath the day after he gave his most famous speech, in Birmingham. It is often called the 'Rivers of Blood' speech, because, as a classical scholar, Powell quoted Roman poet Virgil in saying he saw 'the River Tiber foaming with much blood'. This is referred to in the novel: 'That Powell … with his bloody rivers' (p. 267). Powell used the quote to express his view that immigration was creating social problems that would get worse in years to come. He claimed that many immigrants did not want to integrate. He was opposed to anti-discrimination laws, and wanted to encourage immigrants to return home. This is reflected in the novel: 'If he wants to send us back, let him come and … try!' (p. 267).

KEY QUOTATION: SKINHEADS (A01)

At the fete someone calls Sam a 'skinhead idiot' (p. 194) because of his close-cropped skinhead hairstyle. His gang evolve from being Mods in 'baggy green anoraks with targets painted on the back' to skinheads in 'short denim jackets, tight jeans held up with braces, and huge clumpy boots' (p. 174). The Mods typically wore tight, tailored suits and parkas, had short hair, rode scooters, and listened to soul and ska. Skinheads were a white working-class youth sub-culture that grew out of the Mods in the 1960s. Their style was partly a rejection of the values of long-haired middle-class Hippies. They were known for violence, especially towards ethnic minorities. Their so-called 'bovver boots' were part class style statement, part weapon. Some skinheads identified with neo-Fascism and the right-wing group the National Front.

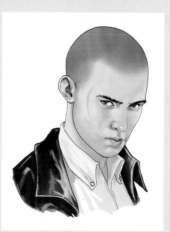

TOP TIP (A02)

Two comments on the novel's back cover (Harper Perennial edition) refer to it being set in the 1960s. The reference to Enoch Powell (p. 267) suggests 1968, and references to money in shillings and pence (pp. 21, 155) suggest a date before decimalisation – which happened in 1971. However, references to the Kennedy assassination (p. 9) and Miss World competition (p. 166) happening when Meena was very young indicate that the novel begins in 1972.

KEY CONTEXT (A03)

Sam's hypocritical attitude can be seen as typical of racists. He fails to connect Meena, an individual whom he likes, with immigrants as a whole.

SETTINGS

KEY CONTEXT (A03)

The Black Country covers an area of the West Midlands to the north-west of Birmingham. It probably gets its name from its high level of sooty air pollution during the Industrial Revolution, though the name may also come from the amount of coal in the area.

Most of the action takes place in or near the village of Tollington. Exceptions are the expedition to the Sikh temple in Birmingham, Meena's four-month stay in hospital, and mentions of other nearby settings in digressions, such as the description of Papa's office Christmas party 'on the outskirts of Wolverhampton' (p. 260). The Kumars and their friends, and Nanima, also talk about India. Here are the key settings in the novel:

- Tollington has 'a row of terraced houses clustered around the crossroads' (p. 11). The houses become 'bigger and grander' towards the south. Then there are 'miles of flat green fields'. Downhill to the north is Mr Ormerod's shop, the Working Men's Club and the primary school, and small terraces – 'two-up-two-downs' (p. 11).
- The 'small overgrown park' (p. 12) next to the Yard is where Meena tries to comfort Anita (p. 247). As the Bartlett estate spreads, the park is taken over by teenagers.
- The Big House is the old mine owner's house. Meena can see its trees from her window (p. 13), and its owner watches Nanima's welcome party from behind his fence (p. 206). Anita takes Meena into the wooded grounds to see a Hindu statue (p. 126).
- The Pembridges' Tudor mansion is 'at the posh end of the main village road' (p. 167). The annual fete is held in its garden.
- Hollow Ponds (also called Hollow *Pond*) are 'the deep water-filled old mine shafts at the back of the Big House' (p. 100). This is where Jodie Bagshot drowned, and where Tracey almost drowns.
- Dale End Farm, on the edge of the village, is where Sherrie lives, where she and Anita ride Trixie, and where Meena breaks her leg (p. 279).
- Mr Ormerod's shop is where Anita shoplifts and Meena steals a collection tin (p. 154).
- The Good Hope Children's Ward (Ch. 12) is where Meena recovers from her broken leg, and gets to know Robert.

KEY CONTEXT (A03)

Miners' tithe cottages were originally owned by the mine owner and inhabited by his employees. They normally had two bedrooms upstairs and a sitting room and kitchen downstairs. The toilet was outside.

TOP TIP: DESCRIBING SETTINGS IN PASSING (A02)

Notice the narrative device used to introduce Tollington and particular settings where action will occur later. Having Papa take Meena to the shop as the novel's first event achieves several things. It starts the novel with action and suspense, introduces Meena, Papa and even Mama, seen hanging out washing, and enables Meena to describe places as she passes them, supplying details about setting in a subtle way. For example, she looks back at her house, 'halfway down the hill, standing on the corner of the crossroads, one of the miners' tithe cottages huddled around a dirt yard' (p. 12).

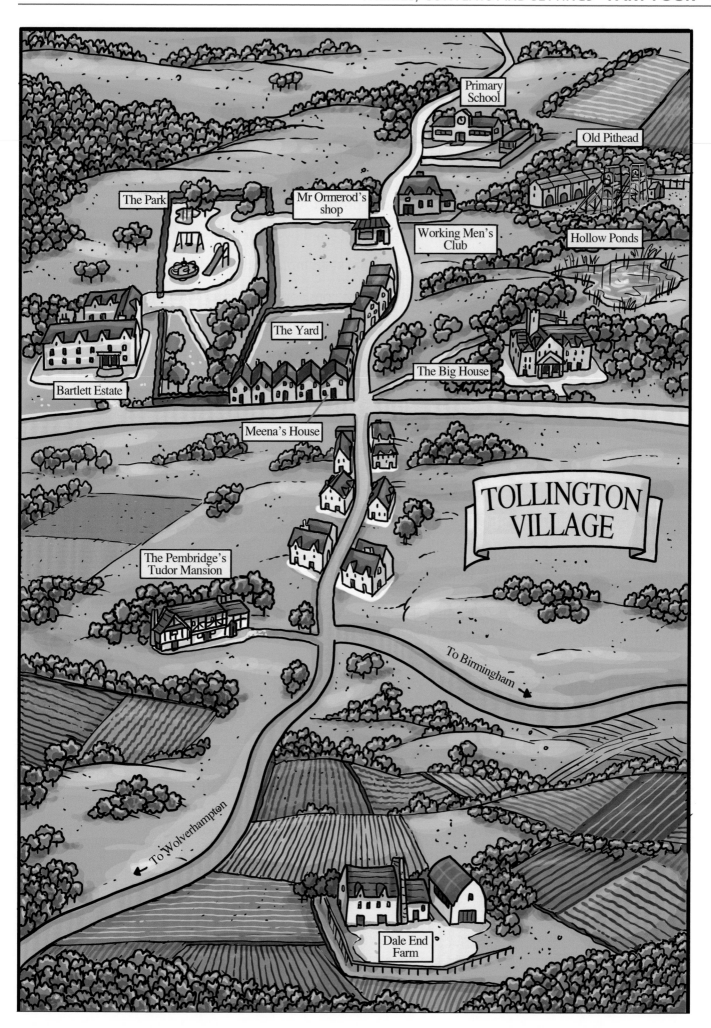

Primary School

Old Pithead

The Park

Mr Ormerod's shop

Working Men's Club

Hollow Ponds

The Yard

The Big House

Bartlett Estate

Meena's House

TOLLINGTON VILLAGE

The Pembridge's Tudor Mansion

To Birmingham

To Wolverhampton

Dale End Farm

PROGRESS AND REVISION CHECK

SECTION ONE: CHECK YOUR KNOWLEDGE

TOP TIP (A01)

Answer these quick questions to test your basic knowledge of the themes, contexts and settings of the novel.

1 How does Anita set the tone for her friendship with Meena from the start?

2 How does Meena protect Anita at the fair?

3 Why is Mama unimpressed by Mr and Mrs Worrall's children?

4 How do the Kumars keep Indian culture alive with their friends?

5 What is Meena's first conscious encounter with racism?

6 Why is Meena's interview with the police a turning point for her?

7 What post-war event in India encouraged emigration, and why?

8 Who gave the so-called 'Rivers of Blood' speech?

9 Where does Meena lose Mama's necklace?

10 What past event occurred at Hollow Pond(s) and how is it almost repeated?

SECTION TWO: CHECK YOUR UNDERSTANDING

TOP TIP (A01)

This task requires more thought and a slightly longer response. Try to write at least three to four paragraphs.

Task: In what main ways has Meena changed by the end of the novel? Think about:

● what she experiences and what mistakes she makes
● how she develops or learns from her experiences and mistakes

PROGRESS CHECK

GOOD PROGRESS

I can:

● explain the main themes, contexts and settings in the text and how they contribute to the effect on the reader. ☐

● use a range of appropriate evidence to support any points I make about these elements. ☐

EXCELLENT PROGRESS

I can:

● analyse in detail the way themes are developed and presented across the novel. ☐

● refer closely to key aspects of context and setting and the implications they have for the writer's viewpoint, and the interpretation of relationships and ideas. ☐

FORM

OVERVIEW

Anita and Me is a **first-person narrative**, with Meena as its **narrator**:

- Although Meena describes her life during a two-year period aged 9–11 and tries to convey what she felt then, the story is told as if she is looking back on her childhood self with adult knowledge, and using adult language.

- The story is told in the past tense, but with many **digressions**, in which Meena breaks off from the main narrative. These can describe specific past events, such as Meena's birthday outing in Chapter 2, or things that often happened, as when Meena comments on her mother: 'she would often pass other Indian women' (p. 26). This is a digression from a digression!

- Syal extends what Meena can describe in a first-person narrative by having her overhear other people's conversations, such as the adults talking at the Kumars' social evenings.

TOP TIP: PLAYING WITH TRUTH AND FICTION (A02)

Remember that the whole novel is fiction, even though it is based on Syal's own childhood. However, Syal on two occasions plays with the idea of truth and fiction. The first is the opening, when she presents one version of her earliest memories, only to comment in the section beginning, 'Of course, this is the alternative history I trot out' (p. 9).

Before this, there are hints that this passage is going to be a fiction within a fiction. Meena says 'You know' as if inviting us to make up her past ourselves. She also exaggerates to suggest **cliché**, as in her parents' 'dusty Indian village garb' and 'tears of gratitude'. The line 'Polish, I think would be quite romantic' makes it clearer that she is making this up, teasing us with her power as an author (p. 9). The fact that this 'alternative history' is one she might use to 'impress middle-class white boys' (p. 9) tells us that she is an adult narrator looking back.

The second occasion is when Meena announces, 'I had been planning a spectacular revenge' (p. 324). In the next paragraph she gives the account she *could* have given the police, even quoting her own imagined lines, 'No, officer, I was too scared to stop them' (p. 325), demonstrating yet again her flair for story-telling.

TOP TIP (A02)

At several points Syal uses the **narrative device** of **foreshadowing** to hint at what is to come. For example, she hints that Deirdre is having an affair, and that someone at the Big House will turn out to be important. In the opening of Chapter 11 she gives strong hints that a disaster is coming.

KEY CONTEXT (A03)

In literary terms, *Anita and Me* could be called a **Bildungsroman** – a coming-of-age novel, in which the main character learns about life and grows up.

STRUCTURE

OVERVIEW

With so many digressions, the novel may seem rambling, even random. However, it is actually more carefully structured than it seems at first reading.

FIRST DAY OF THE HOLIDAYS (pp. 9–79)

This opening section describes the first day of Meena's school summer holidays. It takes 70 pages to complete one day because of the many digressions. These recount past moments of Meena's life, and introduce Tollington characters and the Kumars' friends, the Aunties and Uncles. During this section we learn that Meena longs for personal drama. The section ends with her learning that she has seen Mrs Christmas's dead body.

THE FRIENDSHIP GROWS (pp. 79–130)

This part focuses on the rising action of the development of the friendship between Meena and Anita. The news that Mama is pregnant heralds changes for the Kumars. It is a significant moment when Anita first calls for Meena, and their visit to the fair is a bonding experience. They have fun together, Meena protects Anita from Deirdre's betrayal, and they share an adventure in the Big House grounds which builds to the episode of Mama's near miscarriage.

SUNIL IS BORN – MAMA CANNOT COPE (pp. 131–61)

Sunil's birth gives Meena more time with Anita. The pair start a gang, Meena passively observes Tracey being bullied, and she reaches a moral low point when she steals the collection tin and blames Baby. But her friendship with Anita is at its strongest point.

SETBACKS AND OBSTACLES (pp. 162–279)

These pages track the friendship's decline, beginning with Meena's anger at the spring fete when Anita admires Sam's racist heckling. At this point Nanima arrives and Meena becomes close to her. In the Easter holidays, Meena watches Anita goad Fat Sally into a fight. Anita's dinner visit is awkward, and Anita tries to steal from Meena afterwards. Meena's efforts to comfort Anita after Deirdre leaves are rebuffed. This period ends with Meena's final disillusionment with Anita, and with Meena breaking her leg.

CLIMAX AND RESOLUTION (pp. 280–328)

This final section is a period of intense learning for Meena. She spends four months in hospital, forms her first relationship with a boy, endures Nanima's departure, and sees Tollington changing. This builds to the climax of Tracey's accident, and Meena's realisation that Sam is a rather pathetic figure. During the falling action Meena tells the truth to the police, takes her eleven-plus exam, and prepares for secondary school.

TOP TIP: WRITING ABOUT DEVELOPMENT (A02)

Make sure you can write about how the pace of the novel varies. Most noticeably, the main action moves slowly while there are many digressions, as in the first section. These digressions have the effect of slowing the action but they are entertaining in their own right and help to flesh out both the main characters and the community around them to give a strong sense of people and place.

On the other hand, there are no digressions while the pace is picking up and building to a climax. Notice, for example, that there are none in the section which begins with Meena making an excuse to leave her parents' social evening and slipping out to the fair (p. 118). The action moves briskly on, with Meena meeting Sam, then going on the rides with Anita and sharing the adventure in the Big House grounds, which builds up to the climax of Mama's medical crisis.

TOP TIP (A02)

Anita and Me, like many novels, has a number of smaller climaxes before reaching its main climax towards the end.

EXAM FOCUS: WRITING ABOUT EFFECTS (A01)

Here is what one student has written about the overall development of Meena and Anita's friendship:

> The friendship builds slowly, with Anita dominating Meena, as when they distress Mr Christmas by 'whooping'. The first time that Anita calls on Meena is an important moment, as it shows that Anita is choosing Meena as a friend. The fair brings them closer together, and the friendship is cemented in the fast-paced section when Meena protects Anita from knowing that Deirdre is with 'the Poet', and then when they are chased by dogs.
>
> Sunil's birth means that Meena sees more of Anita. But as the friendship strengthens, Meena's moral standards decline. First she watches Tracey being bullied, then she shows off to Anita by stealing from Mr Ormerod, blaming it on Baby. From this point on, the friendship declines. Meena's anger at the spring fete is a turning point, but this only foreshadows the climax of Meena's final break with Anita at Sherrie's farm.

Fluent analysis and comment on style

Makes a structural point and explains it

Makes a good point about structural development

Relevant use of technical terms to make a point

Now you try it:

Add a further sentence on the relationship. Start: *When Meena is in hospital ...*

LANGUAGE

OVERVIEW

- The language used for Meena's **first-person narrative** conveys the thoughts and feelings of Meena aged 9–11, but it also uses adult phrasing and vocabulary.
- Syal often uses **comic exaggeration**, sometimes in the form of **imagery**, and sometimes involving **irony**.
- The **dialogue** realistically reproduces working-class Black Country speech and the speech of Indian immigrants for whom English is a second language – albeit one spoken fluently.

LANGUAGE DEVICE: NARRATIVE VOICE

What is narrative voice?	The distinctive manner in which the **narrator** tells the story, including **tone** and **register**, through which the narrator's own character is expressed
Example	'His features effortlessly combined those same contradictions of vulnerability and pride' (p. 11).
Effect	Meena here is narrating quite formally from the perspective of an adult who has had time to think about her father in depth.

TOP TIP

Notice the variations in narrative voice between relatively formal and informal registers. Sometimes Syal combines them for comic effect.

Meena narrates the whole novel – with occasional help from people whose conversations she overhears and relays to us. The narrative voice is usually that of the mature adult looking back at her childhood self, but at times Syal conveys a child's viewpoint through language choice:

- 'if he had listened to me in the first place and just given me the … money, I would not have had to steal anything' (p. 21)
- 'I hoped he had left some bruises so I could make him feel guilty after he had cooled down' (pp. 249–50)

Here Syal uses a conversational tone, with an informal register and some **colloquial** phrases. She also does this at times in the adult voice, especially if commenting on her feelings as a child: 'she sounded so calm and grown up I wanted to gob on her T-bar sandals' (p. 156).

Sometimes the adult and child voices even appear in the same sentence, with the adult voice making a **satirical** comment on the child's viewpoint: 'It would serve them right if I did choke on a raspberry poppet and had foaming convulsions right here on the step' (p. 24).

This conveys a childish view of justice, but also uses a sophisticated, adult descriptive phrase ('foaming convulsions') to satirise Meena's desire for drama and attention.

LANGUAGE DEVICE: DESCRIPTIVE LANGUAGE

What is descriptive language?	Language that describes, creating a picture, for example of places, people, or clothes
Example	Mrs Christmas's dresses are 'all delicate flowers, roses and bluebells and buttercups, set against cream silk or beige sheeny muslin' (p. 43).
Effect	The flower names, with the repeated 'and', create a sense of great variety. Subtle colours and fabric names add to the visual effect. The description shows that Meena is impressed enough to notice.

One of Syal's commonest uses of descriptive language is to introduce characters, to bring them alive for the reader:

- Hairy Neddy is 'a plump, piggy-eyed man in tattered jeans'. People 'couldn't quite make out where his beard ended and his mouth began' (p. 47). This paints a picture and creates a faintly comic impression of a man who is rather careless about his appearance.
- Tracey has 'huge red-rimmed eyes' and a 'cowering, pleading look'. She is a 'thin, sickly child ... dark and pinched' (p. 46). The language makes her seem pitiable.

LANGUAGE DEVICE: IMAGERY

What is imagery?	Language that creates a word picture using a **simile**, a **metaphor** or **personification**
Example	Referring to her mother, Meena says, 'It never ceased to amaze me how expertly she rode and reined in my father's moods' (p. 80).
Effect	This metaphor describes Papa's moods as if they are horses that might gallop away unless controlled by a rider who knows them well. It could be seen as **foreshadowing** Meena's riding accident.

TOP TIP (A02)

Always point out the *effect* of any devices you mention: you will not earn credit just by identifying them.

Syal makes frequent use of the different types of image, making the narrative more colourful and adding meaning. For example:

- 'she tugged at her lacquered helmet of hair' (p. 54). This metaphor for Deirdre Rutter's hair (it is not literally a helmet) fits its shape (a 'beehive'), its stiffness, and her self-protective hardness as a character.
- Meena describes her mother: 'her brown skin glowed like a burnished planet' (p. 12). This simile describes her complexion and implies her importance to Meena.
- Meena speaks of her excitement 'when death became possible, visible, bared its teeth and raised a knife in Indian moonlight' (p. 37). This personification makes death more threatening by picturing it as a creature with teeth, wielding a knife.

LANGUAGE DEVICE: COMIC EXAGGERATION

What is comic exaggeration?	Language that makes a point using entertaining overemphasis
Example	Meena describes two women whose 'instinctive reaction was to grow three feet in height, snarl and send death rays to each other (p. 52).
Effect	They sound like a cross between gods, wolves and Martians. It is an entertaining way to say they loathe each other.

Some whole passages are comically exaggerated. For example, Hairy Neddy's car is 'lying in various stages of disembowelment in the yard', like a murder victim. He has attempted a hill 'at fifty miles per hour in second gear'. Another car arrives 'on two wheels', like a speeding cartoon car (p. 48).

LANGUAGE DEVICE: MAGICAL LANGUAGE

What is magical language?	Language expressing a character's perception by describing the impossible
Example	After disgracing herself, Meena imagines Anita, 'laughing in reverberated echo as the heavens slowly crumbled and fell in blue jagged lumps' (p. 115).
Effect	This expresses Meena's confusion at adult disapproval, as well as Anita's unkindness towards her.

Meena dreams that she sees Nanima 'rise slowly into the air and circle the room, her pyjama bottoms flapping like Hermes' wings at her ankles' (p. 207). This suggests Nanima's power – like that of the Greek god Hermes.

Meena's police interview is heralded by a visionary experience: 'I flew right through the roof of my house and I saw everything' (p. 325). This gives Meena the wisdom to know that it is 'time to let go' and tell the truth.

LANGUAGE DEVICE: DIALOGUE

What is dialogue?	Direct speech, expressing character and moving the plot on
Example	Mama finds herself having to give the Mitchells a lift: '"So am yow gooin down the shops then?" they said in unison. "Why, yes," Mama said, still smiling. "Can I give you a lift?"' (p. 113).
Effect	The way the Mitchells seize the opportunity for a lift is comic. They speak colloquially, saying 'down' for 'to'. Syal represents their accent in 'yow gooin' for 'you going'.

TOP TIP

Dialect is a local form of speech that uses non-standard grammar and vocabulary. Accent refers to the way words are pronounced.

TOP TIP (A02)

The local working-class characters speak in the Black Country dialect and accent. For example, a 'piece' is 'a peculiar Tollington word for a sandwich' which Mama calls the language of 'an urchin' (p. 53). Meena uses slang to distance herself from her father (p. 148). The contrast is strongest when Meena threatens Pinky in dialect and Pinky asks, 'Meena didi, why are you speaking so strangely?' (p. 152).

PROGRESS AND REVISION CHECK

SECTION ONE: CHECK YOUR KNOWLEDGE

TOP TIP (A01)

Answer these quick questions to test your basic knowledge of the form, structure and language of the novel.

1 Why does Syal take 79 pages to tell the story of one day?

2 How does Syal introduce us to Tollington?

3 How does Syal get round the problem of the child Meena only being able to recount her own experience?

4 What is the term for the device used at the start of Chapter 11 ('If I had known')?

5 What is the main, and final, **climax** of the novel?

6 In what way are there two **narrative voices**?

7 How does Syal imply Deirdre's character by using a **metaphor** for her hair?

8 What is the main effect of exaggeration in the novel?

9 What device is used to describe Tollington as 'prancing around' (p. 88)?

10 In what local dialect do Meena and Anita speak?

SECTION TWO: CHECK YOUR UNDERSTANDING

TOP TIP (A01)

This task requires more thought and a slightly longer response. Try to write at least three to four paragraphs.

Task: In what ways does Syal make the style of the novel more entertaining than a simple recounting of events? Think about:

- the style which the story is told, and its effects
- how Syal uses narrative devices

PROGRESS CHECK

GOOD PROGRESS

I can:

- explain how Syal uses form, structure and language to develop the action, show relationships and develop ideas. ☐

- use relevant quotations to support the points I make, and make reference to the effect of some language choices. ☐

EXCELLENT PROGRESS

I can:

- analyse in detail Syal's use of particular forms, structures and language techniques to convey ideas, create characters and evoke mood or setting. ☐

- select from a range of evidence, including apt quotations, to infer the effect of particular language choices and to develop wider interpretations. ☐

UNDERSTANDING THE QUESTION

For your exam, you will be answering a question on the whole text and/or a question on an extract from *Anita and Me*. Check with your teacher to see what sort of question you are doing. Whatever the task, questions in exams will need **decoding**. This means highlighting and understanding the key words so the answer you write is relevant.

BREAK DOWN THE QUESTION

Pick out the **key words** or phrases. For example:

> **Question**: How does Syal present prejudice in *Anita and Me*? Write about the different examples of prejudice in the novel and how they are presented.

What does this tell you?

- Focus on **the theme of prejudice** but also on **'different examples'** – **instances** of prejudice and **how they differ**.
- The word **'presented'** tells you that you should focus on the ways Syal reveals these attitudes, i.e. the techniques she uses.

PLANNING YOUR ANSWER

It is vital that you generate ideas quickly and plan your answer efficiently when you sit the exam. Stick to your plan and, with a watch at your side, tick off each part as you progress.

STAGE 1: GENERATE IDEAS QUICKLY

Briefly **list your key ideas** based on the question you have **decoded**.

For example:

- *Elderly woman in traffic queue*
- *Mr Ormerod's patronising attitude*
- *Sam's selective racism*

TOP TIP (A02)

You might be given a question that asks you how particular characters are used to explore a theme – for example, Daljit and Deirdre to explore the theme of family.

STAGE 2: JOT DOWN USEFUL QUOTATIONS (OR KEY EVENTS)

For example:

- 'I backed off as if I had been punched' (p. 97)
- Mr Ormerod: 'It's about giving them culture as well, civilisation' (p. 172)

STAGE 3: PLAN FOR PARAGRAPHS

Use paragraphs to plan your answer. For example:

Paragraph	Point
Paragraph 1	**Introduce** the **argument** you wish to make: *Syal explores the theme of prejudice in a variety of ways, mainly through Sam Lowbridge but also through other characters.*
Paragraph 2	Your first point: *Sam is resentful that society has not helped him to get on in life. He does not want charity to go to foreigners, and he objects to immigrants coming to Britain, especially if they seem to be successful, like the man Sam and his gang beat up and rob – Rajesh Bhatra.*
Paragraph 3	Your second point: *Syal presents prejudice as being caused by ignorance and misunderstanding. Sam does not make the connection between Meena and Bhatra, and fails to see that Meena might be upset by racist heckling. Even Anita is insensitive to this. Sam regards immigrants other than the Kumars as a threat because he does not know them personally.*
Paragraph 4	Your third point: *Some prejudice is less obvious. Mr Ormerod collects money for the African poor, but has a patronising attitude. He thinks people in developing countries should be taught how to live like the English. Even the Kumars' neighbours only accept them because they do not see them as being properly Indian.*
Paragraph 5	Your fourth point: *Syal shows that anyone can be prejudiced. Mama and the Aunties, who have experienced prejudice themselves, in India and England, criticise the family values and personal hygiene of the English, as if they were all the same.*
	(You may want to add further paragraphs if you have time.)
Conclusion	**Sum up** your argument: *Syal presents prejudice across a broad spectrum, from well-meaning patronisation to the violent hatred that human beings can feel for those perceived as alien, whether of a different colour or a different religion.*

TOP TIP (A01)

You may not have time to write such a detailed plan in the exam, but this is a good example of how to structure your ideas into paragraphs. Remember to back up your points with evidence from the text, events or quotations.

TOP TIP (A02)

When discussing Syal's language, make sure you refer to the techniques she uses and, most importantly, the *effect* of those techniques. Don't just say, 'Syal uses lots of adjectives and adverbs here'; write, 'Syal's use of adjectives and adverbs shows/ demonstrates/ conveys the ideas that ...'.

RESPONDING TO WRITERS' EFFECTS

The two most important assessment objectives are **AO1** and **AO2** (except for Edexcel, where you will only be examined on AO1, AO3 and AO4). They are about *what* writers do (the choices they make, and the effects these create), *what* your ideas are (your analysis and interpretation) and *how* you write about them (how well you explain your ideas).

ASSESSMENT OBJECTIVE 1

What does it say?	What does it mean?	Dos and don'ts
Read, understand and respond to texts. Students should be able to: • Maintain a critical style and develop an informed personal response • Use textual references, including quotations, to support and illustrate interpretations	You must: • Use some of the literary terms you have learnt (correctly!) • Write in a professional way (not a sloppy, chatty way) • Show that you have thought for yourself • Back up your ideas with examples, including quotations	**Don't write:** *Anita looks like she's really upset that her mum's gone off.* **Do write:** *When Deirdre leaves, Anita's 'red and crusty' eyes show she has been crying and has not slept. The metaphorical 'snail trails' on her face show she is too miserable even to wipe away her tears.*

IMPROVING YOUR CRITICAL STYLE

Use a variety of words and phrases to show effects:

Syal *suggests ..., conveys ..., implies ..., explores ..., demonstrates ..., describes how ...*

I/we (as readers) *infer ..., recognise ..., understand ..., question ..., see ..., are given ..., reflect ...*

For example, look at these two alternative paragraphs by different students about Anita. Note the difference in the quality of expression:

Student A:

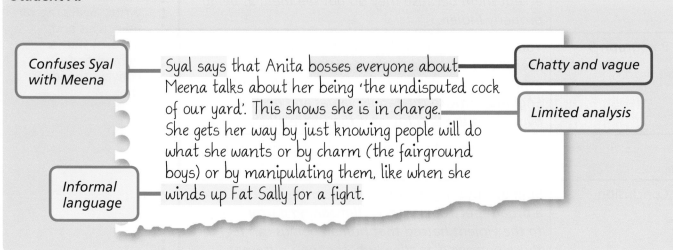

Confuses Syal with Meena

Syal says that Anita bosses everyone about. Meena talks about her being 'the undisputed cock of our yard'. This shows she is in charge. She gets her way by just knowing people will do what she wants or by charm (the fairground boys) or by manipulating them, like when she winds up Fat Sally for a fight.

Chatty and vague

Limited analysis

Informal language

Student B:

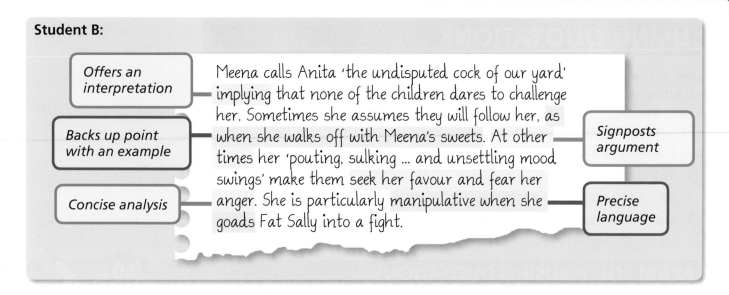

| Offers an interpretation |
| Backs up point with an example |
| Concise analysis |

Meena calls Anita 'the undisputed cock of our yard' implying that none of the children dares to challenge her. Sometimes she assumes they will follow her, as when she walks off with Meena's sweets. At other times her 'pouting, sulking ... and unsettling mood swings' make them seek her favour and fear her anger. She is particularly manipulative when she goads Fat Sally into a fight.

| Signposts argument |
| Precise language |

ASSESSMENT OBJECTIVE 2   **A02**

What does it say?	What does it mean?	Dos and don'ts
Analyse the language, form and structure used by the writer to create meanings and effects, using relevant subject terminology where appropriate.	'Analyse' = comment **in detail** on **particular aspects** of the text or language. 'Language' = vocabulary, imagery, variety of sentences, dialogue/speech, etc. 'Form' = **how** the story is told (e.g. first-person narrative, overheard conversations, notes, chapter by chapter) 'Structure' = the **order** in which events are revealed, or in which characters appear, or descriptions are presented 'create meaning' = what can we, as readers, **infer** from what the writer tells us? What is **implied** by particular descriptions, or events? 'Subject terminology' = **words** you should use when writing about novels, such as 'character', imagery, 'setting', etc.	**Don't write:** *The writing is really descriptive in this bit so you can really imagine what time of year it is.* **Do write:** *Syal emphasises the seasons as an aspect of change. Meena describes her love of spring, **symbolised** by the call of the cuckoo, and **personifies** Tollington as 'prancing around in its ostentatious autumnal cloak' (p. 88). The playful image **expresses** Meena's love of language, as well as **implying** the richness and innocence of childhood.*

IMPLICATIONS, INFERENCES AND INTERPRETATIONS

● The best analysis focuses on specific ideas or events, or uses of language and thinks about what is **implied**.

● This means drawing **inferences**. On the surface, Sam Lowbridge can be seen as a hate-filled racist, but is it that simple? What does the description of him and his gang with 'shaven heads, downy and vulnerable as dandelion clocks' (p. 226) imply?

● From the inferences you make across the text as a whole, you can arrive at your own **interpretation** – a sense of the bigger picture, a wider evaluation of a character, relationship or idea.

USING QUOTATIONS

One of the secrets of success in writing exam essays is to use quotations **effectively**. There are five basic principles:

1. Only quote what is most useful.
2. Do not use a quotation that repeats what you have just written.
3. Put quotation marks, i.e. '…', around the quotation.
4. Write the quotation exactly as it appears in the original.
5. Use the quotation so that it fits neatly into your sentence.

EXAM FOCUS: USING QUOTATIONS (A01)

Quotations should be used to develop the line of thought in your essay, and to 'zoom in' on key details, such as language choices. This **mid-level example** shows a clear and effective way of doing this:

| Makes a clear point | Syal presents Papa as a hard-working man. She says that he came home every day with a 'briefcase full of papers covered with minute indecipherable figures'. This shows how work even dominates his home life. | Gives an apt quotation |

Explains the effect of the quotation

However, really **high-level responses** will go further. They will make an even more precise point, support it with an even more appropriate quotation, focus on particular words or phrases and explain the effect or what is implied to make a wider point or draw inferences. Here is an example:

Makes a precise point

Apt quotation

Explains the effect of language

Syal presents Papa as a responsible, long-suffering father. Meena says he arrives home from work every day with 'a bulging briefcase full of papers covered with minute indecipherable figures'. The phrase 'minute indecipherable' conveys to the reader that, although Meena can make no sense of the figures, she understands the effort her father has to make to provide for the family. Meena's comments on her father show the reader how much she loves him.

Zooms in on a key phrase

Infers meaning to broaden the point

SPELLING, PUNCTUATION AND GRAMMAR

SPELLING

Remember to spell the **author's** name, the names of all the **characters**, and the names of **places** correctly.

Practise the spellings of key terms you might use when writing about the text such as: character, theme, irony, simile, metaphor, imagery, personification, dialogue, etc.

PUNCTUATION

Remember:

- Use **full stops and commas in sentences accurately** to make clear points. Don't write long, rambling sentences that don't make sense; equally, avoid using a lot of short repetitive ones. Write in a fluent way, using linking words and phrases, and use **inverted commas** for **quotations**.

Don't write:	Do write:
Meena is very loyal to Anita though unappreciated as when she stops her finding out about the Poet and her mother and when she tries to comfort her after her mother has gone off and is pushed away.	*Meena is very loyal to Anita, as shown, for example, when she protects Anita from finding out about Deirdre's betrayal with 'the Poet'. Her attempt to comfort Anita when Deirdre leaves is unappreciated: Anita rejects her.*

GRAMMAR

When you are writing about the text, make sure you:

- Use the present tense for discussing what the writer does, e.g. *Syal shows the reader that Sam is not entirely bad: he shows initiative and is 'polite, even kind' to Meena.*
- Vary character names with pronouns (he/her) and use references back to make your writing flow.

Don't write:	Do write:
Despite Meena loving her father, she lied to her father and at one point Meena deliberately used local dialect to upset Papa and distance herself.	*Despite loving her father, **Meena lies** to **him** and at one point deliberately **uses** local dialect to upset **him** and distance herself **from him**.*

TOP TIP (A04)

Spelling, punctuation and grammar may be worth up to 5% of your marks, but even if not examined (e.g. by OCR) you should aim to make your writing as accurate and fluent as possible, to get your points across to the examiner.

TOP TIP (A04)

Enliven your essay by varying the way your sentences begin. For example, *Hairy Neddy eventually proposes to Sandy after ignoring her for months* can also be written as *Having ignored Sandy for months, Hairy Neddy eventually proposes to her.*

TOP TIP (A04)

Syal often uses comma splices to divide sentences to convey an informal, conversational tone, but you should avoid them. For example: *Meena admires Anita, she wants to be like her.* This is grammatically incorrect. It should be: *Meena admires Anita. She wants to be like her*, or *Meena admires Anita and wants to be like her.*

ANNOTATED SAMPLE ANSWERS

This section provides three **sample responses**, one at a **mid** level, one at a **good** level, and one at a **very high** level. This is an AQA-style question which assesses all four AOs. However, it will also be useful for checking your own level if you are following the Eduqas, OCR or Edexcel specifications.

> **Question**: How does Syal present the ways in which Meena changes during the novel?
>
> Write about:
>
> - How and why Meena changes
> - How Syal presents these changes

SAMPLE ANSWER 1

A01 — Gives a minimal introduction, rather jerkily

Meena goes through a lot of changes. The first is in her lying. The story begins with a lie, Papa is taking her to the shop to see if she was really given sweets or if she stole a shilling for them and she admits in the end that she was lying. She admits she lies a lot, like when she tells 'harmless fabrications' like her being a Punjabi princess or 'major whoppers' to get out of trouble. She still does this kind of thing much later, she tells some women that Nanima speaks Russian and is a diamond miner who escaped a volcano. But in the end she gives up lying and tells the truth to the police. This is an important change because she could get revenge on Anita and Sam by saying they threw Tracey in the pond.

A02 — Makes a relevant point and explains its significance

A01 — Leads clearly into the next part of the argument

Meena also changes in her relationship with Anita. She starts out believing whatever Anita says, for example that her dad is a sailor, she also totally admires Anita: 'knowing that I was privileged to be in her company'. This means she thinks she is lucky just to be with Anita. Later she says 'Anita talked and I listened.' But the power balance changes when they go to the fair and Meena protects Anita from knowing what Anita's mother is up to with 'the Poet'. She also shows sympathy for Anita when she sees her mother make her cry and when her mother has gone off and Anita is crying in the park. Meena begins to see that Anita is not just hard and 'cock of our yard'.

A04 — Informal expression and comma splice – should begin new sentence

A02 — Analysis with apt quotation

The friendship goes downhill as Meena becomes more independent. For example, she objects when Anita approves of Sam's racism. Meena stands up for her views at this point.

She eventually realises that Anita needs her more than she needs Anita, and that Anita was never going to get a pony. Meena pities her, but in the end she rejects her for enjoying a racist attack.

A02 Good point, but needs more explanation

Meena also changes towards Sam. At first she thinks he is 'polite, even kind', then she regards him as a racist and stands up to him. In her final meeting with him it seems she has always found him secretly attractive, but now she feels powerful and sees him as pathetic.

A01 Introduces final point well, but ends clumsily

However, the biggest way Meena changes is towards being Asian. All through the novel she identifies more with English culture than Indian. An example is when she sings a pop song at the music evening instead of an Indian song. She even wants to be white and writes to 'Jackie' magazine about it. But because of Nanima, she starts to get interested in India and her heritage.

A02 Makes a good point about Syal's presentation, but not clearly enough

A01 Brief but fairly effective conclusion referring back to the question

With Meena's new sense of belonging in the world, we rely on what she tells us about herself. Losing Nanima and Robert has made her stronger, so she knows: 'the place in which I belonged was wherever I stood.' She does not feel 'displaced' now.

By the end Meena has changed hugely, mostly because of losing Anita, Nanima and Robert. She has come to accept herself and does not need to tell lies all the time.

MID LEVEL

Comment

The understanding of character development is expressed and some sound points are made, though not always clearly enough. Paragraphs are used effectively, but vocabulary is limited and words or expressions repeated. The overall effect is too chatty in tone. The student needs to write in a more formal style and should also discuss the effects Syal creates, referring to literary terms.

For a Good Level:

- Develop a formal critical style, drawing on a wider range of vocabulary and avoid informal language or slang.
- Show how the novelist creates effects with language devices.
- Make sure quotations are embedded in sentences so that when a sentence is read it flows easily and the quotation feels part of it.

SAMPLE ANSWER 2

A02

Makes a clear point, citing evidence concisely and fluently

Meena grows as a character during the novel. At its centre seems to be the question of truth. In the preface the adult Meena tricks us with a fake personal history, which she tells to boyfriends. Then Chapter 1 opens with her pleading, 'I'm not lying, honest, papa.' He thinks she has stolen a shilling to buy sweets – which she has. She also admits to 'harmless fabrications' that make life more interesting, and to more serious 'whoppers' to get herself out of trouble. She is still telling wild stories much later, when she tells the Ballbearings women that Nanima is a mine owner and speaks Russian. Her telling the police the truth about Tracey is an important turning point. It shows she knows that honesty is important at times.

A02

Highlights narrative viewpoint and technique

It is in her relationship with Anita that Meena develops most. At first it is very unbalanced. Meena admires and trusts Anita, for example believing that the sailor in an advert is Anita's father. Later, Anita sets the tone for the friendship by snatching Meena's sweets and going off, knowing Meena will follow. Meena admits that she felt 'privileged' to be in her company.

A01

Develops argument with analysis of example and apt quotation

Anita encourages Meena to be more daring and rebellious, like when they both anger Mr Christmas by 'whooping'. Their going into the Big House woods is an example of Anita making Meena more adventurous, but Meena goes further by going right up to the statue. This happens just after another sign that the relationship is changing: Meena protects Anita from knowing that 'the Poet' is having sex with Deirdre. This shows that Meena cares about Anita, in a motherly sort of way. She also shows that she cares when she tries to comfort Anita after Deirdre has left.

A02

Analyses effect, with interpretation

Meena also changes in how she sees racism, and this affects her friendship. Living in a village, she has been protected from racism, although it was on the increase in Britain at the start of the 1970s. Early on, she is shocked as if she has been 'punched' by the elderly driver who 'casually' abuses her. The image shows how hurt she feels. When she hears Sam's racist heckling she is also shocked, because she saw him as a 'mate', but she has the independence to call Anita a 'stupid cow' for being impressed. This eventually develops into Meena rejecting Anita for boasting about her part in a racist attack. It is as if she makes herself fall from Trixie as a way to break from Anita.

A03

Refers to social context

A02

Analyses structure and offers interpretation

Meena's anti-racism is linked to another way in which she develops: her acceptance of herself and her Indian heritage. This is partly thanks to Nanima, who is a direct link to India and tells exciting stories that make Meena want to go there. Nanima also accepts Meena as a 'junglee', meaning a wild girl. This helps Meena to accept herself and stop wanting to be white like all the girls in Jackie magazine, published before the media became aware of different ethnic groups.

A03 Highlights social context

Meena develops most through 'absorbing' the losses of Nanima, Robert and Anita, 'like rain on parched earth'. This image shows that the losses seemed natural, like she needed them. Syal makes her first-person narrator tell us about this important change herself rather than presenting it through action and dialogue. Her 'sense of displacement ... carried round like a curse' disappears. In the end she is strengthened by suffering and looks forward to her new future.

A02 Analyses an effect

A02 Comments on author's technique, referring to question

GOOD LEVEL

Comment

This is a clear and fairly confident response demonstrating a good understanding of the character's nature and development, and of the novel's context. Language devices and narrative techniques have been highlighted, with some exploration of language to emphasise effects, though there could be more. Quotations are relevant and fluently embedded in sentences.

For a High Level:

- Give more analysis of Syal's use of language, especially imagery, and narrative devices.
- Extend the range of vocabulary, and look for more sophisticated words to express ideas.
- Aim for more consistent fluency.
- Give more thought to an effective introduction and conclusion.

SAMPLE ANSWER 3

AO1
Maps out the essay, relating themes to character

AO1
Correct and relevant use of literary term

Anita and Me is a 'Bildungsroman', a novel about a character growing up, whose title announces its main subject – Meena's friendship with the older, white working-class Anita, which is central to Meena's development. However, she also develops in three other ways: her attitude towards truth and fiction, her attitude to racism, and her attitude to herself as the daughter of immigrants. Syal connects all three to the friendship with Anita.

AO2
Sophisticated point about technique

Even in the preface Syal highlights truth and fiction as a theme, when she uses viewpoint to play with the author's role by presenting a false personal history for Meena. The main narrative starts with a more childish lie – Meena's claim that she did not steal a shilling. She confesses to telling other children stories about being a princess, calling these 'harmless fabrications', but also to telling 'whoppers' to avoid punishment. Much later, she still makes up stories, as when she thinks the Ballbearing women deserve to be tricked about Nanima's background and talents. However, Syal prepares us for the importance of Meena's greatest temptation by giving her a visionary out-of-body experience. She is about to lie to the police, but her experience makes her tell the truth. This shows that she can now be honest when it matters.

AO2
Analyses effect of narrative device

When Meena meets Anita, she believes Anita's lie about her father being a sailor: playing with fiction is something they have in common. When the friendship starts, Anita establishes its terms by walking off with Meena's sweets, correctly assuming that Meena will follow. Anita, as 'cock of our yard', dominates, but Meena gradually becomes her equal, then outgrows her. Part of this process is when Meena mothers Anita, protecting her from what Anita's real mother is doing at the fair. Meena also tries to comfort Anita after Deirdre leaves. Her rejection of Anita begins when she dares to call her a 'stupid cow' for admiring the racist Sam Lowbridge. Although the friendship resumes, Anita's admiration for racism remains an issue. When Meena overhears her lightly calling Sam's 'Paki bashing' 'bosting', this is the end of the friendship. Syal presents Meena's emotional conflict and loss in the dramatic climax of Meena riding Trixie. Meena seems to injure herself deliberately in order to end the friendship.

AO2
Fluent embedding of quotation and analysis

AO2
Analyses narrative impact and offers interpretation

A02 Fluently analyses effect

Earlier on Meena has been shocked by racism, reacting to the elderly driver who insults her as if 'punched', the word choice showing her emotional pain. She reacts similarly to Sam's racist heckling. Gradually, however, she toughens up, standing up to Sam, and accusing Mr Ormerod of cheating Nanima. When she hears of her Auntie Usha suffering the kind of racist attack that was becoming common in the early 1970s, she feels 'both impotent and on fire', the metaphor revealing her powerless passion. But by the time she has her climactic kiss with Sam, she feels 'mighty' compared with him, and is even able to pity him.

A03 Refers to social context

Nevertheless, Meena's greatest change is in her sense of 'displacement' as the child of Indian parents in Britain. She wants to be like the white girls in 'Jackie', but Nanima boosts her self-image as an Asian girl at a time when there were few ethnic role models. After Nanima's return, Meena says she 'absorbed Nanima's absence and Robert's departure like rain on parched earth'. The simile shows she has thrived on her loss, so that her 'displacement' has 'shrivelled into insignificance'. We might think, nonetheless, that the euphemism 'departure' for Robert's death suggests she could not accept it completely.

A02 Analysis of device, using correct term

A03 Refers to social context

A02 Close focus on word choice

A02 Effective conclusion making final point about presentation

Whereas Meena's other changes are presented through action and dialogue, her new sense of self is revealed only in her self-description as narrator, so we have to take her word for it. Despite this, it is clear that her suffering has made her a stronger person, able to be herself, regardless of colour, and to be at home wherever she is.

VERY HIGH LEVEL

Comment

This is an excellent critique of how Syal presents Meena's development. There is thoughtful analysis of literary techniques, language and effects. Links have been made between character and themes. A sophisticated range of appropriate vocabulary and expression has been used and sentence structure has pace and variety. The conclusion completes the argument and includes a sophisticated point about narrative technique.

PRACTICE TASK

Write a full-length response to this exam-style question and then use the **Mark scheme** on page 88 to assess your own response.

> **Question:** How does Meera Syal explore the theme of family in *Anita and Me*?
>
> Write about:
>
> ● The role of family in the novel
>
> ● How Syal presents ideas about family

TOP TIP (A01)

You can use the General skills section of the **Mark scheme** on page 88 to remind you of the key criteria you'll need to cover.

Remember:

● Plan quickly and efficiently by using key words from the question.

● Focus on the techniques Syal uses and the effect of these on the reader.

● Support your ideas with relevant evidence, including quotations.

FURTHER QUESTIONS

1. 'Sam and Anita are presented as victims of society.' How far is this true in *Anita and Me*?

   Write about:
   ● In what ways they are, or are not, victims of society
   ● How Syal presents their characters

2. How does Syal explore the importance of culture in *Anita and Me*?

   Write about:
   ● Examples of culture in the novel
   ● How these examples are presented

3. Read from 'There it is ...' (p. 126) to 'our smiling elephant god, Ganesha' (p. 127).

   With close reference to the extract, show how Syal tells the story in an exciting way here.

4. In what ways do Anita and Meena have a positive influence on each other in the novel?

LITERARY TERMS

alliteration	repetition of the same sound at the beginning of words close to each other
atmosphere	the mood created by a setting
Bildungsroman	a coming of age or 'education' novel that describes one person growing up
cliché	a widely used expression which has lost impact through overuse
cliffhanger	a device that ends a chapter in the middle of a dramatic event, leaving the reader anxious to discover what happens next
climax	the part of a narrative with the greatest emotional tension
colloquialism	a casual form of expression used in speech
comic exaggeration	comedy that achieves its effect by making something seem more extreme than it really is
descriptive language	language that creates an impression of a thing, setting or character, especially using adjectives
dialect	non-standard vocabulary and grammar used in a particular area
dialogue	the words spoken by characters in conversation
digression	text which departs from the main subject or narrative thread
euphemism	a more pleasant or sanitised way of saying something unpleasant or offensive
extended metaphor	a metaphor that likens the thing described to something else in several different ways
falling action	the final stage of a novel, after the main climax, when the narrative winds down and concludes
first-person narrative	a story told from the viewpoint of one character, using 'I'
foreshadow	when an author hints at what is to come
imagery	creating a word picture; common forms are metaphors and similes
irony	saying one thing while meaning another, often through understatement or indirect statement
magical language	language that describes the impossible happening
melodramatic	characterised by sensationalism, passion and extreme action
metaphor	a figure of speech describing something, someone or an action as something else in order to imply a resemblance; e.g. 'the drum of [Trixie's] belly' (p. 278)
narrative	a story, a series of connected events
narrative device	a technique used to tell the story, such as Meena overhearing
narrative voice	the way in which the narrator's character is expressed
narrator	the voice telling the story
personification	when things or ideas are treated as if they were people, with human attributes
register	the choice of vocabulary and sentence structure used for a particular purpose, especially formal or informal
rhetorical question	a question asked to make a point rather than to receive an answer
rising action	when the plot and action develop towards the climax
satire	writing which ridicules something using ironic humour
setting	the place where events occur, often used to create atmosphere, reflect a character's feelings, or symbolically
simile	a figure of speech using 'like', 'as' or 'than' to compare
stream of consciousness	writing in which a character's thoughts follow in a loose, dream-like way as ideas flow into each other
subordinate clause	part of a sentence, usually separated off by one or more commas, that only makes sense in relation to the rest of the sentence; e.g. 'Meena, who is nine, lives in Tollington'
symbol	something used to represent something else, often an idea or emotion
tone	how the narrator or a character speaks; can also be set through description
unreliable narrator	a biased or untrustworthy narrator
withholding information	in a narrative, concealing information for dramatic impact and to arouse curiosity, usually to reveal it later

CHECKPOINT ANSWERS

CHECKPOINT 1, p. 12

- Mama wants to show the English that Indian women can dress tastefully and speak perfect English.
- Mama is critical of English food.
- Sandy thinks it is a compliment to say that Mama seems English.
- Some English members of the community worry about the apparent size of the Kumar family.
- The Indians criticise English gardens, family values, morality and personal hygiene.

CHECKPOINT 2, p. 15

- Anita dominates, expecting Meena to feel privileged to be with her – which she does.
- Anita encourages Meena to be more daring and rebellious.
- Meena is respectful towards adults; Anita is not.
- Anita wants to carry on seeing Meena, even though Deirdre seems to disapprove.

CHECKPOINT 3, p. 22

Meena is:

- beginning to learn about sex and courtship, from Anita and *Jackie* magazine.
- worrying about the consequences of her lies.
- starting to experience racism and realise that her parents have coped with it.
- becoming rebellious – as when she refuses to take off the make-up.
- becoming closer to Anita, and protective towards her.
- behaving badly, as when she steals the collection tin and blames Baby.
- increasingly identifying with non-Asian culture and values.

CHECKPOINT 4, p. 25

- It is spring, and women are spring-cleaning, perhaps signifying change.
- Meena sees Sunil as a nuisance.
- There are plans for the M6 to be built nearby.
- The fortune-teller predicts a dilemma for Meena and trouble for Anita
- There is talk of growing racism, underlined by Sam's heckling.

CHECKPOINT 5, p. 27

- Nanima takes the pressure off Mama by helping with Sunil.
- She is like a second mother to Meena and accepts her 'wild' side.
- She makes Meena interested in India and her cultural heritage.
- Meena tries to learn Punjabi to communicate with her.
- Meena develops a sense of responsibility towards Nanima.

CHECKPOINT 6, p. 28

- Deirdre claims not to have a job, but is out all day (p. 90).
- She comes home 'flushed, bustling with secrets' (p. 90)
- She pulls 'the Poet' into his caravan (p. 122).
- She has had a violent row with Roberto (p. 133).
- She arrives home in an unfamiliar car and kisses a man goodbye (p. 206).

CHECKPOINT 7, p. 31

- Meena takes it to make herself look grown up, though she hides it under her vest (Ch. 5).
- Meena loses it in the Big House grounds, when fleeing from dogs (Ch. 5).
- Mama finds the necklace is missing and at first suspects Anita (Ch. 11).

CHECKPOINT 8, p. 33

- Meena forms her first relationship with a boy – Robert.
- She realises that Anita does not care about her: she never visits.
- She learns that her actions have consequences: the family cannot go to India.

CHECKPOINT 9, p. 34

- She has lost her role as an only child.
- Nanima has returned to India without her.
- Robert has died.
- She has lost Anita as a friend, perhaps to Sam.

CHECKPOINT 10, p. 40

Meena:

- says Ormerod gave her the sweets, when in fact she stole a shilling (Ch. 1).
- says she is going to the toilet, but sneaks out to the fair (Ch. 5).
- claims to know nothing about Mama's missing necklace (p. 267).
- steals the collection tin from Ormerod and blames Baby (Ch. 6).
- claims Nanima is a multilingual mine owner, and fled a volcano (pp. 220–1).

CHECKPOINT 11, p. 42

- Anita chooses friends she can dominate – and Meena is younger than her.
- Deirdre makes her cry.
- She believes (or claims) that she is going to be given a pony.
- She seems to believe that 'the Poet' cares for her.
- Meena can see she has been crying in the park after Deirdre leaves.

CHECKPOINT 12, p. 44

Papa:

- tries to teach Meena not to lie, and gives her opportunities to tell the truth.
- tells her stories.

- is sensitive to the fact that she may be upset by Robert dying.
- makes an effort to be friendly to Anita.
- works hard to support the family.

CHECKPOINT 13, p. 46

Shaila:

- recalls losing her sister during Partition (p. 74).
- is 'the fattest, noisiest and most fun' of the Aunties (p. 74).
- is critical of Sunday School.
- has a Hindu shrine on her fridge and tells Meena about reincarnation.
- tells Meena to remove her make-up.
- comments on Meena's singing.
- protects Meena when Mama almost miscarries.
- furiously punishes Pinky and Baby.

CHECKPOINT 14, p. 47

- Deirdre makes Anita cry.
- Anita seems to be afraid of her.
- She gives Anita money at the fair so that she can spend time with Anita's 'boyfriend'.
- Tracey seems neglected.
- Deirdre eventually abandons the family.

CHECKPOINT 15, p. 52

- Meena listens to Anita.
- She protects Anita from Deirdre's betrayal at the fair.
- She is kind to Anita when Deirdre leaves.
- She does not tell anyone that Anita shoplifts.
- She writes Anita a pleasant farewell note, despite having reasons to resent her.

CHECKPOINT 16, p. 56

- Sam's racist heckling.
- Sam's TV publicity stunt.
- Sam's gang beating and robbing the Indian man.

PROGRESS AND REVISION CHECK ANSWERS

PART TWO, pp. 36–7

SECTION ONE

1. He wants to know if Meena stole money to buy sweets; 2. A religiously motivated murder by a rickshaw driver in India; 3. Mr Christmas, because it may disturb his terminally ill wife; 4. A criminal record; 5. In India, when he was a teenager; 6. Diwali, in late October; 7. A lift to the shops; 8. The Wenches Brigade; 9. Mr Pembridge, in whose garden it takes place; 10. Replacing the chapel roof; 11. Deirdre Rutter; 12. Punjabi; 13. Sherrie's farm; 14. Anita's mother has walked out on the family; 15. He rides his moped at reporter Gary Skip and shouts into the TV camera; 16. Trixie; 17. Her memory of Anita; 18. Nurse Sylvie; 19. Her feet – the one that had the plaster cast on is smaller; 20. She throws herself at Sam to protect Anita from him, but misses.

SECTION TWO

Task 1: Possible Plan

- Meena despises Pinky and Baby's obedience, their 'matching outfits' and 'cutesy plastic bobbles' (p. 151), and even their Punjabi accents. She feels superior to these 'infants'.
- She only reluctantly takes them to the shop. She is ashamed of them and worried that they will show her up in front of Anita.
- Meena is dishonest, cruel and bullying when she makes Baby hide the stolen collection tin, but she is delighted by Anita's admiration for this. Later, she enjoys the sisters' 'fear and bewilderment' because it reaffirms that she is 'nothing like them' (p. 158).
- Worst of all, Meena has no shame in putting on an act and blaming Baby for the theft, so that both sisters are punished – showing that she can be extremely selfish.

Task 2: Possible Plan

- Sherrie notices Anita's bra and Anita shows it off: she is proud of growing up. When Sherrie feels one of the straps, Tracey reacts protectively. When Anita pins Tracey against Trixie's stall, this makes Tracey accuse Anita of letting 'him' touch her (p. 276). Sherrie guesses that Anita has a boyfriend. Anita's smile confirms this.
- Meena feels jealous and betrayed: 'I knew whatever she had been giving me was only what she had left over from him' (p. 277). She reacts like a jilted lover.
- Syal uses the device of Meena overhearing Anita to reveal that the boyfriend is Sam Lowbridge, and that Anita was with him when he attacked the Indian man and loved it – 'it was bosting!' (p. 277): she is an ignorant racist.
- Meena's response is to endanger herself by riding Trixie. It is as if she wants to kill her emotional pain by getting herself injured: 'all I had to do was make something happen' (p. 279).

PART THREE, p. 50

SECTION ONE

1. A Sunday School; 2. Hairy Neddy; 3. Anita tells Meena that the sailor in a Capstan cigarette advert is her father; 4. Papa finds that Meena has lied about stealing money for sweets; 5. Papa is shocked to see Mama trying to move a settee when she is heavily pregnant; 6. Nanima; 7. How to make jam tarts; 8. Anita sees Sam kissing Meena; 9. Deirdre Rutter; 10. Meena: Anita has been crying because her mother has left.

SECTION TWO

Possible Plan

- Anita encourages Meena to be more adventurous, for example at the fair and in the Big House grounds, and to be more rebellious.
- She gets Meena interested in boys, by her own example, by telling her about sex, and by providing copies of *Jackie*.
- She gives Meena a sense of being accepted by at least one friend, although she also makes Meena want to be English and white.

- The fortune-teller tells Meena, 'You are under a bad influence, but you cannot break free' (p. 185) and that Anita is not her friend (p. 186).
- Anita encourages Meena to shoplift and lie, putting the blame on Baby.
- She unintentionally teaches Meena lessons about friendship, by being disloyal, racist, and not visiting her in hospital.

PART FOUR, p. 62

SECTION ONE

1. Anita shows her dominance by snatching Meena's bag of sweets and walking off, expecting Meena to follow; 2. Meena prevents Anita from knowing that Deirdre is in a caravan with 'the Poet', probably having sex with him; 3. Mr and Mrs Worrall's children never visit them, though they do not live far away; 4. The Kumars have musical evenings where they perform Indian songs and *ghazals*; 5. Meena asks an elderly woman to reverse her car, and she replies with racist abuse; 6. Meena could get revenge on Anita and Sam by saying they pushed Tracey into the pond, but she chooses to tell the truth – that it was an accident; 7. The 1947 Partition of India into India and Pakistan led to widespread violence, mostly between Hindus and Muslims; 8. Enoch Powell; 9. The Big House grounds; 10. Jodie Bagshot drowned there and Tracey Rutter almost drowns there.

SECTION TWO

Possible Plan

- Meena begins the novel as a liar: she lies about stealing money for sweets. Later she behaves even more badly, blaming her own theft on Baby. When Anita comes to dinner, Meena tells a 'white lie' to make everyone feel more comfortable. Finally, she tells the police the truth, implying that she has now learnt the value of honesty.
- Meena moves from simply admiring Anita and wanting to be like her, to feeling pity for her and realising her faults and weaknesses – her insecurity and need to fantasise, and even her ignorant racism.

- She develops a sense of responsibility – for example, towards Nanima, towards her own parents, and towards her brother Sunil.
- She learns that her actions have consequences – as when she breaks her leg.
- She finds a new sense of contentment, losing most of her sense of displacement, as a result of her relationships with Nanima and Robert, and surviving their loss.

PART FIVE, p. 69

SECTION ONE

1. Because so much of the text is made up of digressions, including descriptions of Tollington; 2. Syal has Papa take Meena to Mr Ormerod's shop, which allows Meena to describe the village as she passes through it; 3. She has Meena overhearing other characters' conversations; 4 Foreshadowing; 5. The scene in which Tracey throws herself at Sam and falls in the pond; 6. We hear the voice of 9–11-year-old Meena, and the voice of her adult self looking back; 7. Deirdre's 'helmet' of hair implies that she has a self-protective hardness; 8. Exaggeration is used for comic effect; 9. Personification; 10. Black Country.

SECTION TWO

Possible Plan

- There are many digressions describing past events and providing insights into Meena's character, such as when she nearly chokes on a sausage (p. 27). Similar digressions reveal local characters, such as Hairy Neddy.
- Meena recounts stories of India that she overhears or is told by Nanima.
- Syal uses a great deal of imagery and vivid descriptive language to bring the story to life, as well as comic exaggeration. These are entertaining in themselves, and they add to the sense of narrative voice that reveals Meena's character.

MARK SCHEME

POINTS YOU COULD HAVE MADE

- Meena has loving, nurturing parents. They encourage her to behave well and work at school.
- The Kumars miss their extended family. They tell Meena about them. When Mama cannot cope with Sunil, Nanima comes to support her, becoming like a second mother to Meena.
- The Kumars make a new 'family' of the Aunties and Uncles.

- Anita's family is dysfunctional. Syal hints that Deirdre is unreliable, implying that she is dangerous. Then Deirdre abandons the family.
- Tracey is neglected and probably abused.
- No relatives visit the Christmases
- The Worralls' adult children never visit.
- Syal contrasts Indian and English family values, especially through Mama's comments.

GENERAL SKILLS

Make a judgement about your level based on the points you made (above) and the skills you showed.

Level	Key elements	Spelling, punctuation and grammar	Tick your level
Very high	**Very well-structured answer which gives a rounded and convincing viewpoint.** You use very detailed analysis of the writer's methods and effects on the reader, using precise references which are fluently woven into what you say. You draw inferences, consider more than one perspective or angle, including the context where relevant, and make interpretations about the text as a whole.	You spell and punctuate with consistent accuracy, and use a very wide range of vocabulary and sentence structures to achieve effective control of meaning.	
Good to High	**A thoughtful, detailed response with well-chosen references.** At the top end, you address all aspects of the task in a clearly expressed way, and examine key aspects in detail. You are beginning to consider implications, explore alternative interpretations or ideas; at the top end, you do this fairly regularly and with some confidence.	You spell and punctuate with considerable accuracy, and use a considerable range of vocabulary and sentence structures to achieve general control of meaning.	
Mid	**A consistent response with clear understanding of the main ideas shown.** You use a range of references to support your ideas and your viewpoint is logical and easy to follow. Some evidence of commenting on writers' effects, though more needed.	You spell and punctuate with reasonable accuracy, and use a reasonable range of vocabulary and sentence structures.	
Lower	**Some relevant ideas but an inconsistent and rather simple response in places.** You show you have understood the task and you make some points to support what you say, but the evidence is not always well chosen. Your analysis is a bit basic and you do not comment in much detail on the writer's methods.	Your spelling and punctuation is inconsistent and your vocabulary and sentence structures are both limited. Some of these make your meaning unclear.	